KNAPTON REMEMBERED

KNAPTON REMEMBERED

Edited by

GILLIAN SHEPHARD

Larks Press

Published by the Larks Press in association with
Baroness Gillian Shephard

Printed by The Lanceni Press
Fakenham, Norfolk

October 2007

British Library Cataloguing-in-Publication Data
A catalogue record for this book is available
from the British Library

Front Cover: Knapton Sports Team at North Walsham 1949
Back row: Betty Wright, Shirley Wright, Avril Edwards, Barbara Dixon, Janet Woolsey,
Willie Puncher, John Rayner, Brian Puncher, Derek Miller, Russell Woolsey
Front Row: Jill Watts, Yvonne Lee, Janet Steward, Margaret Wild, John Wild, Brian
Eastoe, Michael Miller, Brian Watling.

ISBN 978 1 904006 39 8

ABOUT THIS BOOK

The idea for this book came from a letter written by Michael Miller to the *Eastern Daily Press* in November 2006. The letter was headed 'Watts not Betts' and said 'Re. London Diary (EDP November 3rd), unless my memory has failed me, Gillian Shephard's single name was Gillian Watts when we both attended Knapton School together.' When I read that letter, whose purpose had been to correct an error in the article concerned, I rang Michael. As a result of our conversation, and after a lot of work by a lot of people, this book was born.

I contacted Janet Steward (now Munro), and June and Richard Wild, who still live in the Knapton area, to see if they thought we might have a reunion of former Knapton pupils, and whether we might ask people to record their memories of their time at the school, and of the village. They reacted enthusiastically, and agreed that it might make sense to concentrate our attention on the period at the school as headmistress of Mrs Johnson, 1934 to 1961, when sadly and prematurely she died in office. Although we have concentrated on that period, some of our contributors pre-date it.

We decided that a useful way to start would be to ask former pupils to complete questionnaires about their time at Knapton School, and if they wished, to provide a written account of their memories. To help people remember events in their past, I compiled a list of 'memory joggers' which, while they may have been helpful to some, have in no way limited what people have written. A copy of the letter, the questionnaire, and the memory joggers is to be found at Annex A.

Janet, June and Richard worked very hard on the project from the start. They vetted the questionnaire and memory joggers, and made useful suggestions and changes. They got into touch, tirelessly, with former Knapton pupils, provided names and addresses, and put people in touch with one another. They helped distribute questionnaires to others, booked the village hall for the Reunion, held in April 2007, and themselves provided a substantial amount of the material in the book. June's account of the history of the Men's Club is a model of its kind, as is Janet's description of the role of the Methodist Chapel in Knapton. They worked as a team, and have at all times remained great supporters of the project. They have been equal partners, and nothing would have happened without their help.

Jenny Wild (now Lambert) also offered advice and ensured that members of her family came to the Reunion. Pearl Hicks (now Eves) and Linda Fawkes (now Risebrow) prepared the hall and provided refreshments for the day itself. Pearl Hicks also gave us the interesting history of

Knapton Chapel, written by her father, Herbert Hicks. This is to be found at Annex D.

Kathleen Johnson (now Suckling) the daughter of Mrs Johnson, the inspirational head of Knapton School during the period covered, provided invaluable research on her mother's career, and an insight into how this remarkable woman managed family, career, and public service.

John Rayner had already written an extremely interesting account of his life, and this book contains relevant extracts from that account.

Four people have written about subjects of which they have expert knowledge. Pamela Dixon (now Garnham) has written about the village shop, which her parents, and then she, ran, and about the changes in shopping habits which eventually led to the shop's demise. Willie Puncher still lives and farms on the farm where he was brought up. He describes changes in farming over the past 60 years. June Wild's history of the Men's Club compiled by her from the Minutes of the Club Committee starting in 1938, gives a vivid picture of the way things were run in the village. Janet Steward (now Munro) explains the role of the Chapel, and writes about her famous uncle, Arthur Amis, Methodist, Labour activist, union man, councillor, and himself a former pupil of Knapton School.

The descriptions of life in the school and the village are vivid, whether they form part of the questionnaires, or in the written accounts. While there is obviously some overlap, all give a personal picture of lives lived sixty or more years ago. To them, whether they wrote a personal account, completed a questionnaire, or attended the Reunion, we owe a big thank you. They are the authors of this book. The names of all the people involved with the project are listed at Annex B. The occupations of their parents, and details of their own subsequent careers, where these have been provided, are given at Annex C.

My husband Tom, who went to school in Devon, has, despite that, taken a great interest in our work, and put in hours on the computer to get the manuscript into a fit state for the publisher.

Susan Yaxley of the Larks Press is married to David Yaxley of the family which appears in this book. She has worked meticulously to prepare the book for the press

Much more could be written. Many of us feel we have only scraped the surface of our memories, and what they tell us about our own lives and the history through which we have lived. But we have made a start, and what we have written will be saved for our children, our grandchildren, and future generations of people in Knapton, in Norfolk and much further afield.

Contents

Reproduced from the (1954) Ordnance Survey Map Sheet 126
Crown Copyright 1954

INTRODUCTION

Knapton is a small village, of around 300 people, one and half miles inland from the North Sea at Mundesley, and about four and half miles from the nearest market town, North Walsham, in North East Norfolk. Arthur Mee, in Norfolk, the King's England Series published in 1940, says that 'its road leads uphill past scattered dwellings, a mile and a half from the sea, and the tower of its 14th century church is a landmark and a magnet, drawing us to one of the finest treasures of its kind in the land' – a reference to the extraordinary double hammer beam roof in the church dating from 1503.

During the period covered by this book, 1934 to 1961, Knapton had a school, the church of St Peter and St Paul, a Methodist Chapel, a variable number of shops and an equally variable and reducing number of farms. There was no pub but there was a station. Trains passed through the Knapton and Paston station on their journey between North Walsham and Cromer Beach station.

What has emerged from the accounts of Knapton and its school between 1934 and 1961, recorded in this book, is a vivid picture of a community, isolated and close-knit, with many inter-related families. We learn that the principal occupation is agriculture but with other supporting trades and professions, like carpentry, agricultural engineering, and blacksmithing. Surprisingly, we also learn that many of the women work, some on the land, others in domestic and other work. We read of what people ate, how they lived, their preoccupation with daily chores, like getting water, lighting fires, and doing the washing. We learn what enjoyment was to be had from village social life, and the role played by church and chapel. There are some strange gaps in people's memories; for example, there is almost no mention of ill health, or visits to the doctor, nor indeed of the introduction of the National Health Service in 1948. Nor is there much mention of local or national government. On the other hand, there are many references to those who were perceived as running the village, notably Miss Robinson, and her companion, Miss Leather, the rectors, Reverends Prichard and Thur, Mr May of Church Farm, Mr Cargill, who owned Old Hall Farm, Major and Mrs Wilkinson, Dr Gutch, Mr and Mrs Hicks, Ursula Fawkes, and others.

The importance of the school, and of its inspiring head teacher, Mrs Johnson, illuminates every page. The school was small, not more than between 30 and 40 pupils except when evacuees swelled its numbers during the Second World War. Yet pupils were given as broad an education as was possible given the obvious constraints, in a way which would not shame the most modern of today's schools. The extra-curricular activities, like trips to London and to Blakeney Point, the visits to other schools for sports, singing and dancing events, are all described. Mrs Johnson's love of the environment in which Knapton is set, and the pageant of the seasons with their occasional extremes of weather, also emerge clearly.

What is particularly interesting about people's memories as revealed in the questionnaires and written accounts is their perception of enormous historical events. What we have in the book is a series of grass roots views of the Second World War, and its repercussions on families, and normal family lives. The period encompasses nothing less than a series of revolutions in agriculture, the economy, transport, shopping, prosperity and opportunity, all of which are commented upon as they affect everyday life. In this period, children experienced at first hand, although not necessarily consciously, the introduction of the 1944 Education Act, statutory provision of school meals, and the raising of the school leaving age in 1947.

Sadly, the book also describes the demise of a thriving and almost self-sufficient community. Knapton today has no school, no station, no shop, and only a handful of farms. In that respect, it resembles countless other communities, changed for ever by progress. That same progress has meant that no child today, nor any in the future will have what we had, absolute freedom to roam the fields and woods of our village, secure in the knowledge that we would be safe, nor the security of the predictable annual sequence of events. However, not all progress is bad. Memory and distance enhance what at the time must have been hard, tough, and sometimes cheerless. But what we hear in this book is the voice of childhood, and we see our village through the eyes of its children, with all their optimism and joy. And we hope that that voice, that optimism and that joy will come through the decades to our readers, whoever they may be.

PART 1

In many ways, Mrs Johnson was the inspiration for this book. We begin, therefore, with this account of her extraordinary life by her daughter, Kathleen Suckling.

Mrs Kathleen Johnson 1901 -1961.

My mother was born in Bradford, Yorkshire, in November 1901, the elder of two daughters. Her parents both worked at Lister's Woollen mill. I am not sure what my grandmother's job was but she may well have been a 'mill girl' along with her inseparable friend Maud Steele. My grandfather was a linguist having been educated at Bennet College in Sheffield. This, I think, was run by a charity for bright boys from poor families. He was fluent in several European languages and corresponded with a German and a French man for many years. He dealt with the foreign business for Listers. On one occasion a Chinese visitor came to Bradford and my grandparents were asked if they could entertain him during his visit. Unfortunately my grandfather's skills did not cover Mandarin and my grandmother told me that they spent the time making signs and smiling and bowing to each other. My grandfather was not a well man and died in his thirties in May 1915.

My mother, too, was a bright child and was doing well at a local school when she was struck down with appendicitis when she was nearly 15 in the autumn of 1916. She was among the early survivors of the pioneering operation but was advised that her only hope of returning to anything like full health was to leave the city and spend a quiet life in the country!

In the meantime Maud Steele had met and married Walter Priest and was living in Fakenham. I am not sure if my mother came to Norfolk on her own to stay with them or if her mother and sister came as well. Certainly they were all living in Fakenham a few years later on. To aid her convalescence my mother delivered newspapers for one of the Priest brothers who ran a stationery firm and printing works in Fakenham.

After some time my mother had evidently recovered and started work as a shorthand typist in Fakenham Post Office, where she soon achieved a high shorthand speed. During the 1920s the Priest brothers also ran the cinema in a hall in Fakenham. My mother and friends ran the box office. They also helped the pianist as this was the era of silent films. The pianist had her music sorted into piles according to various situations and the helper had to be ready to hand over the appropriate music for the scene being shown! They also had to help with PR when the projector broke down or the film was damaged, refunding the clients their money.

Also during the early 20s my mother had a holiday in Bordeaux with my grandfather's French correspondent and family. Monsieur Pivert was a wine merchant and shipper. She told me about wine tasting sessions and having to spit the wine out into large spittoons. (His grandson, Edmond, visited Knapton in the 1950s.)

At some point she started work as a pupil teacher at Guist. The story goes that she bought a bicycle to make the 10 mile journey each way to and from Fakenham. She took her teaching certificate by correspondence course from Norwich Training College and started as a Supplementary teacher at Colkirk School in January 1922. She qualified as a teacher in 1927 with a salary of £141 p.a. She moved to Great Massingham C. of E. School in 1928, moving on to Fakenham Girls' Council School in July 1929. Her appointment at Knapton School as Head Teacher was dated 1st December 1933, when the average number in the school was 34.

Mrs Johnson (right) and Mrs Featherstone (left) with the Knapton School sports team in 1957

PART 2

Material from the Questionnaires

Some people chose not to write accounts of the school and village, but instead to give details of their memories in the questionnaires. What follows has been taken from the questionnaires, and in some cases is repeated in the written accounts. Some clear themes emerge.

With regard to the school, there are many tributes to Mrs Johnson, who was head teacher from 1934 until her death in 1961. Mrs Featherstone, who was the infant teacher at the school for many years wrote 'Mrs Johnson was a first class head, years ahead of her time, with the school trips and many other activities that she organised.' Willie Puncher (1942 to 1951) describes her as 'the best teacher one could ask for.' Jacqueline Skippen (1952 to1955) writes 'I went to schools at Honingham, Mundesley, Knapton and North Walsham, and I can honestly say that Knapton was my happiest and most memorable. Mrs Johnson was an absolute inspiration.'

Other teachers were not so popular. Miss Walwark, an infant teacher was remembered by many, in particular by Roy Fawkes, (1934/5 to 1946). He describes Miss Walwark as 'a nasty spiteful, cruel teacher. One Friday afternoon she just left the classroom, she didn't wait for the end of the class, just after lunch she packed her bag and left. I think she thought she would get a rough send off from the children and parents.' Llewellyn Kirk (1935 to 1940/41), on the other hand, says that 'Miss Walwark used to give a Gibbs tooth paste to the top of the class each week.' Anne Lee (1941 to 1947) recalls Miss Doughty, who became Mrs Woodage during the war, 'being in love and then getting married.' Many, including John Rayner, remember Miss Collier, who used to ride to Knapton from North Walsham on an extremely high bicycle each day, whatever the weather, and her strict and old fashioned expectations. Sadly her career was to end after an awful road accident in which she was knocked off her bicycle, an accident witnessed by several of her former pupils, as they cycled to their secondary schools in North Walsham.

Mrs Featherstone writes of the many activities Mrs Johnson organised for her pupils. These included annual trips to London by coach, trips to Cromer for the infants, and excursions to Blakeney Point where pupils saw seals and sea birds, and where the muddy conditions of either the outward or return trip featured strongly. Willie Puncher (1942 to 1951) describes the London trips. 'We went to London by Starling's bus accompanied by Mr and Mrs Johnson and the teacher from the Little

Room. The bus would leave Knapton at 6.30 a.m. We stopped at Newmarket about 9.30 a.m. to stretch our legs and spend a penny. We got to London between 11 and 11.30 a.m. and once there we would visit 2 or 3 places of interest. We moved about London on the Underground. It was really great, we always got on the tube train very quick, we did not want to get left behind. The last place we visited was London Zoo. Once there we could go where we liked as long as we got to the main gate by 6.30 p.m. as that was the time the bus left for home. On the way home, we stopped at Newmarket for some chips or a bottle of pop. We got back to Knapton about 11 o'clock. A lot of us took ten shillings i.e. fifty pence, for spending money. Out of that we had all we wanted, pop, chips, sweets, and plenty of ice cream and a little something for mother. How things have changed. In 2006 I was charged £2 for one ice cream.' Anne Lee also loved the London trips. 'I remember a violent thunder storm when we were in the Tower of London, and my new red shoes ruined my white ankle socks. I remember seeing the Giant Panda, and buying the brooch for my mother at London Zoo.'

Mrs Johnson made sure that the pupils took part in collective activities in the North Walsham catchment area. Many of them, including Mervyn Fawkes (1933 to 1942) recall taking part in singing festivals, on one occasion at St Andrews Hall in Norwich. Others remember sports and country dancing events held at other schools. Ruth Steward writes of a trip on the Broads at Wroxham with Mrs Johnson rowing the boat. This was a reward for passing the eleven plus or Scholarship, to go to North Walsham High School.

Mrs Johnson was very enthusiastic about what would today be called environmental education. Many recall nature walks, including Anne Lee who remembers 'nature rambles down Green Lane by the railway station, pressing flowers and naming them, seeing owl pellets, catching butterflies, caterpillars, Wallage's pond for frog spawn and so on.' Janet Steward (1943 to 1950) writes 'During the spring and summer term we worked in pairs to collect wild flowers. I was teamed up with Margaret Wild, we did better than anyone else. In our allocated week we collected over 100 different species. Each one was put into a meat paste jar (labelled) and then put onto a long shelf on the wall behind Mrs Johnson's desk in the Big Room.'

School lessons were augmented and made interesting by the inclusion of some lessons from the radio. 'Singing Together', 'Dylsford', and 'How Things Began' were mentioned by, among others, Kathleen Johnson, Roger Dixon, Barbara Puncher and Anne Lee.

Another interesting project Mrs Johnson organised at the school was to twin the school with a Scottish fishing trawler. The post–war years marked the height of the herring trade at Great Yarmouth, and several, including Janet and Ruth Steward, write of what they learnt. Janet says 'We adopted a fishing trawler. It came from Buckie to Yarmouth each year. We were allowed to clamber all over the boat, no health and safety then. None of the fishermen on this particular boat could swim.'

In addition to outside lessons for formal PT, and country dancing, plus running, high jump, long jump and rounders, some remember playground games like hop scotch, tig tag, skipping, fivestones and marbles. These games came round seasonally, and emerged at certain times of the year, for no apparent reason. Jokes were told and re-told. Boys played conkers in the autumn. Before Guy Fawkes' Day lanterns for candles were made by hollowing out mangolds or swedes, but there were no fireworks until the late 1940s, and the celebrations were limited to bonfires, and making dampers.

Regular visitors to the school, like the school nurse, the school doctor and the school dentist, and the attendance man (Mr Rix) are recalled by many. The dentist arrived in a van which was a mobile surgery. His visits were unpopular, not only for the obvious reason that he was the dentist, but also because he had breath which smelt of cigarettes, described by Anne Lee. Josephine Watts says that after seeing the dentist she was 'sent home from school with a note to have a tooth out. My mother said no, and I still have the tooth!'

Many enjoyed school, and mention sewing, knitting (boys as well), making things in woodwork, stencilling cards and calendars for Christmas, making paper chains and other decorations to trim the school. Several including Willie Puncher (1942 to 1951) mention that on Thursdays the older boys, from the age of 13, were taken by bus to Southrepps School for woodwork lessons, a concession to the imminence of the raising of the school leaving age in 1947. Years earlier, Queenie Bane (1922 to 1930) writes 'I used to go to Mundesley School for cookery lessons by horse and cart. The boys did carpentry.'

But life outside school was also full of interest. As one might expect in a Norfolk village between 1934 and 1961, the land, the seasons, and gardening loom large in everyone's memories.

Almost everyone, in either written accounts of village life, or in answers to the questionnaires, included memories of agricultural life. Many like Ray Pearman (1936 to 1942) went on to work on the land.

Ray says that he 'worked all my life on farms, leading horses in fields, and milking cows at night.' The father of Ivy and Grace Burlingham (1938 to 1947) and (1942 to 1948) was a farm manager, and their mother worked not only at home but also on the farm sometimes. Both girls helped on the farm also. Grace writes that she fed chickens and pigs morning and evening. Anne Lee remembers the drama of the harvest field, and killing mice and rats as they were forced out of their ever-diminishing haven in the centre of the field. Philip Almey (1946 to 1947), who still farms with his sons at Antingham, was brought up on Poplar Farm in Paston. He remembers work on the farm 'and plenty of it' while he was still at school. Llewellyn Kirk's father was a farm worker before the war, and Llewellyn describes working on Wallage's farm as a 'holdya' boy. He adds, 'We used to have a card with twenty half days off school during the war, for which the farmer had to sign.' Barbara Puncher (1947 to 1961) helped on her uncle's farm washing eggs and can remember steam threshing at Mr Guyton's farm (formerly Wallage's farm) Ruth Steward (1947 to 1953) and Mary Steward (1954 to 1960) both remember going with their father, a farm worker, to Mr May's stackyard when the threshing engine was there. Ruth writes 'Queenie the steam engine and tackle came to Mr May's farm. The stackyard was close to our house. Our goats used to be tethered there, but had to be shut in when Queenie came!' Mary Steward writes 'I used to spend days on the farm when Dad was drying the corn. I was allowed to undo the string on the sacks. I thought it was a very important job.' David White (1954 to 1960) whose father was a pig man 'worked on Saturdays for Mr A. Dixon in his chicken battery farm and the Street.' (Mr Dixon also owned the village shop and post office.) Cecil Yaxley (1947 to 1957), whose father also worked on the land, had also worked as a boy for Mr Dixon 'mainly collecting eggs from his various hen houses, then washing them and traying them up for delivery. We had a huge orchard garden with a few hens and a dog. We used to go beating every Saturday for 2/6d. Nowadays they get £25 but we loved it. My brother, Robin, and I used to follow the threshing tackle, Gooch from Bacton, mostly on Purdy's land. We used to have a stick and try and get the mice as they ran out of the stacks. We would be with them all day, seemed great fun then.' Josephine Watts (1948 to 1956) may have a realistic view when she says of helping in the harvest 'I think we drove Mr May's men mad in helping them.' Neville Coe (1954 to 1960) did fruit picking in the summer to earn money and helped on Mr Hammond's farm (formerly Mr May's). Llewellyn Kirk was 'a member of the British Rabbit Council, and took best in show twice in Mundesley and District Rabbit Show, and also fourth in the Norwich and All England Show with a Siamese Sable rabbit. When we moved to South Wales (after the war) I had to sell the lot, about 50 different breeds of rabbits. My name used to be in the Fur and Feather Book as an accredited breeder.' He also helped at funerals, carrying the planks and tapes back into the church, 'for a bag of sweets.'

Gardening was important as the produce was vital to help feed large families. Gardening was encouraged at school. Behind the school were plots gardened by the pupils, working in pairs. The gardens were judged each year at the end of the summer term, by some of the school managers, as they were then called, including the Rev. Prichard, Mrs May, and Mr Leeder. Michael Miller (1943 to 1952) liked gardening, and remembers his school garden being judged the best in the school. At home, he helped look after 'a large garden, plus a one and a quarter acre field, where sugar beet was grown.' The family kept ducks and guinea fowl. Some lessons were held out of doors, like PE and country dancing which always took place in the playground with a wind-up gramophone. When it was hot, we were allowed to read sitting on the lawn next to the gardens. This was very popular, partly because there was a lovely red may tree, remembered by Jacqueline Croxon, and also because when Mrs Sinkins' pinks were out, we were bathed in fragrance. However, the pinks also represented work, because each year we had to pick and bunch them, and then take them round the village to sell for school funds, 3d and 6d a bunch. Willie Puncher has different memories of the school gardens. He writes, 'In the spring before the digging started, we had to take wheel barrows to collect chicken muck from Mr Johnson's chicken hut on the Mundesley Road, phew what a stink!'

The weather was important to everyone in such a rural community. People have vivid memories of big weather events, such as the snow in 1947, and the floods in 1953, when a hundred people in Norfolk died, some of them on the coast very near Knapton. Mrs Johnson had a block graph to show the prevailing direction of the wind (south west) and each morning a boy was asked to go out to look at the weather vane, and to fill in that morning's block on the graph. When there were high gales we sang 'Eternal Father Strong to Save,' and prayed for people at sea, which was only a mile away. Llewellyn Kirk writes that he remembers 'the snow in 1941 when my cousin and I dug a path through the drifts from the pond down to the Mundesley Road. They brought the farm workers and soldiers to clear the roads. There was a double decker bus. All you could see was the top of the roof in the drifts.' The snow in 1947 lasted for at least 6 weeks, and for part of that time, the school was closed because it could not be heated. Some lessons were arranged in the Parish Room to keep things going. There were real problems for the dairy farmers in the village, as they could not get their milk away, and government bureaucracy made difficulties for it to be sold locally. There were always anxieties about the harvest, and there was a universal sense of relief when we got to the harvest festival services in the church and the chapel. 'All is safely gathered in' had real resonance for us all.

The answers to every questionnaire included references to helping in the house, garden or allotment at home and to other sorts of paid work. Electricity did not come to Knapton until 1948, and running water about a decade later, so cleaning and washing, especially for big families, represented a lot of work where everyone had to help out. Roger Dixon (1938 to 1945) had to get water from the well daily for his family and for Mrs Adeline Watts, in whose garden the well was situated. Anne Lee (1941 to 1947) who was a member of a big family and whose mother was a widow, writes 'We all had our chores to do about the house. Fetching water from the pump at Number 8 or from the well at Number 3 was a regular job for us, as it was needed for washday, bath nights etc. Polishing the lino, cleaning window sills, and steps and using the whitening block on them, preparing vegetables, general errands to the shop or to get accumulators filled in Mundesley all had to be done.' Joan Puncher (1949 to 1957) writes 'We all helped Mum and Dad, cooking, cleaning, washing, getting coal and wood in for the fire, getting eggs and milk from the farm. I helped at the Old Hall, baby-sitting and cleaning at weekends for Mr and Mrs Macmillan. My brother had to fill the buckets with water from the well before he went to school in the morning.' Most families shared a well or pump with others, and every drop of water had to be carried. Lighting was provided by oil lamps, and heating by coal or wood fires. Cooking was in some cases done on a kitchen range, but nearly everyone recalls their mother cooking on an oil stove. For baking, a tin oven was placed on top. Joan Puncher's mother used a wall oven. 'Sometimes the food was burnt on one side.' In Neville Coe's family, there was an open fire and a paraffin oven in the shed. Toilet arrangements were described by many. Obviously the lavatory was in the garden, and its contents had to be emptied, as Neville puts it, 'in the garden on Friday nights! Later on the honey cart passed through the village.' An important and regular job was seeing that accumulators for wireless sets were topped up regularly. They had to be taken to and collected from Mr Bridges in Mundesley.

The dates of this project, 1932 to 1961, obviously encompass the war. People's memories of the war depend very much on their age at the time. Llewellyn Kirk remembers hearing the outbreak of war being announced on the radio, and running round to tell the neighbours, Lou and Adeline Watts. Many in Knapton were in a reserved occupation, namely agriculture, although some enlisted. Kathleen Johnson's and Roger Dixon's fathers had served in the First World War. Roger Dixon's maternal grandfather lived in the USA, and he remembers the family receiving food parcels from him. Leslie Watts, father of Brian, Josephine and Patrick Watts, went into the Royal Navy. Jack Watts, father of Gillian Watts, went into the Marines, although he was called home when his father died suddenly, to look after the family business. Tommy Coe, Neville's father served with the Royal Norfolks, and his mother made shells at Coopers in Kings Lynn. Mervyn and Roy Fawkes' father was a Special Constable, their sister Megan served in the WAAFs, and their brother Ronald was in the Fire Service. Jacqueline Skippen's father was in the armed services during the war. Brian and Richard Wild's father was in the Royal Engineers. June Wild's father was in the Royal Artillery. David and Sylvia White's father was in the Royal Service Corps as a driver. He travelled to France, Italy and Algeria. Sylvia White says that her mother was in the Navy also. Cecil Yaxley's father was in the Army. The family of Anne and Yvonne Lee was involved in various ways. Their elder sister, Daphne, was a land girl on a farm in Trunch. Anne remembers the end of the war 'because my brother would be coming home at last, soon, I hoped. My mother tied our hair in rags to create ringlets for the celebration party, and I had a pretty dress made of blue and white muslin. The siren that was used to herald a raid or all clear eventually became a fire signal, but some months after the war we were collecting rabbit food when the siren sounded and we tore home at break-neck speed, crying "The war is on again", and we were not easily pacified.'

Mrs Johnson, in addition to her full time job as head mistress of the school, joined the WVS, as did Maureen Kirk's mother, Nellie. There was a Home Guard in the village. Llewellyn Kirk's father was in charge of it. Sam and Phyllis Meffin's father was in the Home Guard, as were the fathers of Kathleen Johnson, Willie Puncher, Janet, Ruth, and Mary Steward, William Stubley, Brenda Wilkins and John Wright. Others' fathers were in the ARP, including Ivy and Grace Burlingham's father, and Pamela and Barbara Dixon's father.

Knapton itself was not bombed, although a bomb fell in the field along the Mundesley Road, where the crater can still be discerned.

Philip Almey who lived in Paston at the time can remember shrapnel flying past his back door and getting lodged in a farm gate, from which it was never removed. The beach at Mundesley became a no go area being closed by barbed wire. The adjoining cliffs were mined, in case of invasion. Most people remember German planes going over to bomb Norwich, and hearing bombing raids on Yarmouth.

People can clearly remember food rationing, and the infamous Woolton Pies being made available at Wallage's farm. Llewellyn Kirk remembers having a pie once a week 'as it was on ration' from Mundesley, and finding 'a piece of wire in it. My mother took it back but they would not change it.' He also remembers Ministry of Information films being shown in the Parish Room. When asked what meal they regarded as a treat, some said Christmas dinner, the majority said chicken, others said salmon, goose, and steak and kidney pie. Given the sugar restrictions during the war, many thought that anything sweet, jellies, blancmanges, iced biscuits, and cakes, were a treat, and their consumption tended to be restricted to parties and other treats.

Those who were children at the time have clearer memories of food restrictions being relaxed after the war. Yvonne Lee remembers having her first taste of a banana at Gillian Watts' home. Gillian herself remembers being hugely disappointed by the taste of a banana, having expected it to be juicy. Malcolm Wild remembers his early experience of ice cream, supplied by Payne's Ices from North Walsham in a van marked 'It takes pains to get Paynes' Ices.' Barbara Puncher remembers Dairyland Ice Cream vans coming round, and taking a dish to the van to be filled. Others remember the orange juice and malt supplied through the school, collecting rose hips and waste paper and other salvage for the War Effort. Mrs Johnson was a great enthusiast for National Savings and the school took part in all the activities associated with the drive for the national economy.

Before the war, and the 1944 Education Act, school dinners were not officially supplied, and most children went home at lunch time. Some however came from a distance, and were allowed by Mrs Johnson to bake potatoes on the fire. She herself, with the help of some of the older girls, provided hot meals for those who could not go home for a period until the law was changed, and dinners had to be provided. They were then cooked in the school towards the end of the war by Mrs Watling. After that they were brought from Bacton School in containers, and served by Miss Townsend. They were greatly appreciated, and most people point out that they enjoyed them, especially the chocolate pudding and chocolate custard, which seems to have been a particular favourite. Grace Burlingham (1942 to 1948) remembers 'having dinners in the Big Room and helping Mrs Johnson with them.' Neville Coe (1954 to 1960) says that the 'dinners were good, even the rice pudding.'

Milk also looms large. Queenie Bane, who was at Knapton School from1922 to 1930 says that the children had milk 'sometimes'. Mervyn Fawkes, who was at the school from 1933 to 1942, says that 'there were no dinners but we had milk'. Most people who were at the school during and after the war remember that milk came in little one third of a pint bottles, and that in cold weather these were stood on the fireguard to thaw out. On some occasions, for whatever reason, milk came, not in bottles, but in large cans, and was poured out for the children by Miss Townsend. The milk was definitely variable in freshness according to the weather, and flavour according to what the cows were being fed at the time. Sugar beet tops did not enhance the pleasure of milk drinking, fish meal even less.

Like the written accounts, the questionnaires reveal a rich and varied village life, with regular events which were greatly looked forward to. Fêtes and socials were held to raise money for various causes, like the church, the Christian Endeavour youth group run by the Methodist Chapel, and the Men's Club. Barn dances were held regularly to support the Men's Club, and one was organised to celebrate VE Day. There were dancing classes in the Parish Room. Ivy Burlingham (1938 to 1947) remembers a Pamela Beales 'who came from Norwich to dance for us. She went to Hollywood.' Others mention the pancake socials held in the Parish Room on Shrove Tuesday, when there was a great deal of silent competitiveness between the women who were cooking and tossing their pancakes on oil stoves on the stage for all to see.

Llewellyn Kirk in his written account describes the shops in the village. Knapton is 4 miles from the nearest town, North Walsham, one mile from Paston, where there was also a village shop, and a little further from Mundesley, a village seaside resort with a number of shops including a chemist, and two bakeries. Many goods were delivered, as Anne Lee recounts. 'The fish man came in a van on Friday, and rang a bell. The butcher delivered on a bike with a big front tray, once a week. Mr Gray from North Walsham came with a van with groceries on a Monday and you ordered for the following week when he came with a delivery. We used to copy him saying 'What can I get you, anything large or small?' We would also walk or bike (if we had one) to Mundesley to shop or go to the village shop. A great deal was produced at home. Mother was a great cook and made jam, chutney and pickles.' Brenda Wilkins (1946 to 1952) remembers her family's groceries being delivered by Mr Francis from Paston.

Most questionnaires mention Miss Robinson, the squire or lady of the village, and her car, a Lanchester. They also mention other village leaders, who included Mr Norman May, Mr Henry Wild, and Mr William Wild. The vicar, Rev. Prichard and his car (registration number CPW 440) are remembered by many. The most vivid account of the way the village functioned is given in June Wild's history of the Men's Club, based on its minutes starting in 1938 to be found on page 146 of this book. The fact that her account, based as it is on the records of the club, encompasses the war, but barely mentions it, is particularly telling. The life of the village itself, as revealed by the questionnaires, is rich and self-contained.

Miss Cissie Robinson at Knapton House in the late 1950s

PART 3

What follows is a series of personal accounts which appear in chronological order. Although Alfred Yaxley pre-dates the period covered by this book, his account is so interesting and well written, and mentions so many of the families which appear later, that we have included it in full.

ALFRED GEORGE YAXLEY
at Knapton School 1905 to 1914

Chapter 1

I was born March 17th 1900. In later years as birthdays came round my father invariably reminded me that he had to walk through a snowstorm to fetch the doctor for my birth. It was only a few years before he died in his 89th year that he revealed he spent the rest of the evening in a pub. I was born in his mother's house, he probably felt he would only be in the way if he went straight home. Quite a contrast when my own son was born, I hardly dare leave the house for five minutes at a time. Still things went at a more leisurely pace in those days and father probably thought he needed a pint or two to fortify himself for the two-mile walk home - and for what he might find at the end of the journey. What he found was me.

My Christian names are Alfred George. The George part came from my mother's brother. Alfred, as I found out later, was given to me in deference to the wishes of one of my father's sisters; she happened to be courting a young man whose name was Alfred. Mother told me he was a dapper young fellow who worked in a jeweller's shop. When I asked what happened to Alfred mother casually said 'Oh he jilted her.'

One of my first memories is of King Edward VII's coronation celebrations. I can remember running about in a meadow and seeing tables full of green and red wine glasses, that's all. My mother afterwards told me that there *had* been coloured glasses on tables at the village celebrations. I was only just over two at the time, but I still have the picture in my mind to this day.

Another memory is of a stubble field after harvest. I was walking along holding the hand of a girl with long black-stockinged legs; we were going to see the turkeys, she told me. The hedge was festooned with the red berries of bryony. Where this happened I don't know except that it was somewhere around my mother's home at Thurton.

21

Knapton School children celebrating the Coronation of George V in 1911

I have several other brief memories of this period but strangely enough I can't remember going to school for the first time and hardly anything of my time in the Infants' room except falling in love with a girl named Amy. That must have been towards the end of my time in the Infants' room because I could write a bit and I had the urge to write a love letter to Amy, but the only paper I could find in the house was a piece of Quaker oats package. I can still see the words 'Dear Amy' on the greyish inside part of the packet. I took it up to school but hadn't the courage to hand it to Amy. Poor girl, she never knew I loved her so deeply. The village school was only about 150 yards from the old thatched cottage where we lived. The school consisted (as I suppose it does today) of the Infants' room and the 'big room' as we called it. The infants' teacher was a Miss Lambert who was there when I started and I believe eventually retired from there many years after. The Governess was Mrs Cooper, a plump middle aged widow who lived in the school house with her son and one of her brothers. She had no great learning but was full of commonsense with the ability to teach the three R's, and I think there were few pupils who left that school who couldn't read and write with a fair degree of competence. She wasn't, I suppose, a harsh disciplinarian but I don't remember any children who played the fool in school. Her 'cane' came into play on occasion, it was a thick brown polished piece of wood about eighteen inches long and might have been part of a walking stick. I had it twice during my time at school, once for dirty hands (caused by throwing green tufts of grass pulled from the playground) and once for talking in class. She caned the hands only and always went very red in the face while doing it, so I suppose it hurt her as much as it did us. To me Mrs Cooper was a real good-living woman and I never knew her to be mean and spiteful to a living soul.

The other teacher in the Big Room was a much younger person, or persons, as we had two or three changes in my school days. One in particular stays in my memory. She was a relief teacher named Miss Melts. I remember her in a long tight-fitting mauve dress. She was quite good looking and knew it. She was probably a very good teacher but she always seemed to have a 'down' on me which I didn't care for at the time, but I have often thought since she may have been justified in her views of me; or perhaps at one time she may have been jilted by an Alfred.

I should explain that the school also took a number of children from a nearby village [?Paston] and at one time a feud broke out between the boys of the two parishes. I suppose I was about seven at the time. The older boys looked huge creatures to me but naturally enough I supported the boys from my own village and wanted to do my bit. Being small myself my thoughts turned to weapons of war. I found a piece of wood with a knob at the end. Through this knob I drove several long nails, which made it a fearsome thing indeed. Next morning, armed with this weapon, I trotted proudly off to school wondering if I would get the chance to use it. Fortunately a big boy, one of our own side, saw what I'd got in my hand, smiled very kindly and said 'You know Alfred I shouldn't try to use that, it's too dangerous'. I respected the boy very much and immediately threw my creation to the top of a tall thorn hedge, and that was that. The feud lasted for about another week; then the Governess got to hear about it and stopped it at once, and for the remaining years of my schooldays I don't recall a single instance of bad blood between the boys of the two villages.

Classes were called Standards in those days, and I progressed from standard to standard until I reached standard 6 or 7 - I forget which - when something happened which might have altered the course of my life, but didn't. At that time I was crazy about the Navy and the sea. The Governess got to hear of it, had a talk with my mother, and I was entered for a scholarship which, had I won, would have got me a place on a training ship called *Mercury*. Only two places were allotted to the county of Norfolk. To help me on my way the Governess arranged, and paid for, a course of postal tuition for me. It was frightful agony for me, mainly for this reason. So far as I can remember we never had lessons on grammar at our school. This seems incredible but if we did I can remember nothing. Anyhow, part of this course consisted of grammar and I never really understood any of it. To this day all I know about grammar is that noun means name. Verbs, past tenses etc. are as much a mystery to me now as they were then.

However I did my best to learn, and on the appointed day trudged the three and a half miles to North Walsham for the examinations. On my way there doubts about the whole thing crept into my mind. Did I really want to go to sea? Was I doing the right thing? In fact I took the coward's course, didn't try very hard, chose the easiest subjects (for so doing, the Governess gave me a piece of her mind later) and felt thoroughly miserable about the whole day's work. The results came through later. I had failed to get into the top two - actually I came fifth in an entry of ten.

In later years I often wondered what would have become of me had I won. I have consoled myself by thinking that I would probably have lost my life in the 1914-18 war. Who knows? It may be a matter of interest to say that I made several attempts to join the Navy later on, but it was not to be.

During the last year of my schooldays in standard 7 I did very little work except read. Mostly I chose to read a book entitled *Battles which won the Empire*. Of course my favourite story was the battle of Trafalgar. I never grasped the strategy of it all, but the ships and their names fascinated me. We had a lane in the village called the Green Lane. Part of it had big trees on either side and I named every tree after Nelson's ships, and for years after I could walk along that lane and remember the name of every tree. *Victory* of course was a magnificent oak. Besides being a beautiful tree, it had the added attraction, for me at least, of having a small apple-tree growing from its trunk about four feet from the ground. I never knew whether it was a seedling or a graft, but many years later I saw that it had sent down a root to the ground partly inside the bark. The root then was about the thickness of my thumb, but I haven't seen it since.

I left school when I was fourteen in March 1914, but my liberty was short-lived. I had no job to go to and after a week at home I was hauled back to school. How this came about I never really knew. I suspect it was arranged by my parents and the Governess. Anyway I stayed at school until May 1914 when I found a job.

Chapter 2

It may be just as well to write about the things children did to keep themselves amused when not studying inside the school, and at holiday times. Children in those days had no ready-made entertainments; we had to create our own pleasures and I must say that I can never remember being bored through having nothing to do.

Our games and pastimes always came along about the same dates each year, and it has always been a puzzle to me why it should have been so. I never remember any talk among children about when we should start playing so and so. Take marbles for instance. About the first week in February each year a boy would turn up with a bag of marbles and in a couple of days the marble season would be in full swing. It was the same with the other games. The one exception was pop guns. The start of that season depended on when the acorns began to fall and the date of that varied a bit from year to year. Pop guns could be bought at the village shop for a penny. They were always painted red and a string and cork attached; they were alright for little boys and possibly for a few girls, but were poor things in the eyes of seasoned pop gun warriors. They made their own, or said they did. I rather suspect that most of them were made by their fathers (as mine was) or elder brothers. Mostly they were made from a straight piece of elder wood about nine inches long with the pith bored or burnt out to make the barrel. The stick was made from softer and more seasoned wood which would easily tow. I can't easily explain this 'towing' business. Roughly, it made the end of the stick look like a golliwog's head of hair. The most common method of making a tow would be to spit on the end of the stick, hammer it against a wall, spit and hammer again and again until it had a nice lump at the end. Acorns were usually put in at each end of the barrel, bitten off and flattened against a wall. The stick was then pushed into the barrel a trifle and then pushed sharply in with the flat of the hand or by the chest. That's the best I can do to explain the mechanics of pop guns. If you don't understand it make one yourself and learn by experience. We got the most glorious 'pops' and in time could aim for a target *and* hit it. During the pop gun season the school and village walls looked ghastly from towing and acorn marks, but rain soon washed these away.

The pop gun season suddenly ended and out came the hoops. I have seen hoops made of wood, but mostly they were of iron and made by the village blacksmith. My hoop cost sixpence so I suppose that was the usual price. The thing with which you controlled the hoop was a piece of thick wire or thin iron attached to a wooden handle. The metal end was hook-shaped. To get the hoop going, you stood it upright, gave it a bang with your hand or the hoop iron, and off you went, controlling its direction with the hook. Bowling hoops was, to my mind, one of the most beneficial and exhilarating pastimes a child could indulge in, especially in the winter time. I can still hear the sound of hoops clanging in the village street – one of my most pleasant memories.

I have already mentioned marbles. The school playground would soon be ringing with shouts of 'splits' or 'no splits', 'donkums' or 'no donkums', 'nudgems' or 'no nudgems', and several other terms I can't remember. On the way to school or on the way home we used to play 'traceums'. You threw a marble on the road a few yards ahead of you, you opponent threw another to try and hit yours, and whoever scored a hit pocketed his opponent's marble. 'Traceums' was usually played with glass alleys which were bigger than ordinary marbles and made a better target. Marble playing in the ordinary way i.e. with a hole in the ground could often mean that you could go home with a full bag or none at all. If you or your opponent ran out of marbles you wouldn't lend each other marbles, you would 'donk' them. I dare say our rules and terms were not used in other parishes, but they are as I remember them and who can argue with me now? The marble craze usually died out as suddenly as it came and some other pastime would be taken up.

It was only after the playground had dried up a bit in the spring that we were allowed to play football, usually with a tennis ball. Matches between selected teams would often start on a Monday and end on a Friday, playing that is at playtime and dinner hours. The Governess rather frowned on football – it cut up the playground too much – and sometimes we were forbidden to play for a week at a time in wet weather.

We played another game with cigarette cards, called 'flickums'. The contestants stood a certain distance from a wall, placed a cigarette card between the first and middle fingers and flicked it so as to hit the wall, the art being to hit the wall so that the card fell as close to the wall as possible. The winner took the lot. There were variations which I have forgotten, but like marbles one could go home at the end of the day with a whole lot of newly won cards or none at all.

We played cricket of a sort at school, usually with one set of wickets and one bat, all home made. It was never really popular with all the boys but some of us played, and like a football match started on a Monday and finished on a Friday. I once made 40 runs, which pleased me, but I shall never forget the thrill I had when the innings ended (caught off the school roof) and a boy of my own team came and solemnly presented me with a pencil sharpener in honour of the occasion. Since then I have often had gifts for services rendered but I don't think anything has given me so much pleasure as that little old pencil sharpener, it was so totally unexpected.

Conkers took its place in our games list and I suppose will always be played as it was then, but strangely I can't remember where we got them from. I can't recall a single horse chestnut tree in our village but there must have been some, unless they were imported from the next village whose boys attended our school. I know plenty of horse chestnut trees in that place.

Chapter 3

Our village had a population of 364. I know this because it said so on the cover of the Church Magazine, which was published monthly. During the whole of my school life the population figures of each parish in the Deanery never varied and this used to puzzle me. Eagerly each month I would look for a change in the figures, but no, there it would be, the old familiar 364. I hadn't heard of census counts.

We had, of course, a parish church, a Primitive Methodist Chapel, and the church rooms, commonly known as the Old School, which in fact it was. My father did his schooling there and paid, so he told me, threepence a week for the privilege.

There was the Hall, the Old Hall, the House, and one or two large and very nice farmhouses, a blacksmith's shop, a carpenter's shop, and two grocer's shops. We had two shoemakers who really were shoemakers as well as repairers. Bread and meat were brought in from other places, usually by horse and cart.

The church, like most Norfolk churches, was very big with an inside roof of carved wooden angels. I was told when a boy that those angels were taken from a ship wrecked along the coast a few miles away, but I have since read that this was not the case. What the actual facts were I can't remember. The font has a Greek inscription on it which reads the same either way. My father and mother were church people and we were brought up as members of the church but my grandmother, my father's mother, was a Primitive Methodist and as likely as not I would go with her to chapel on Sunday afternoons or evenings. I must say I have more pleasant memories of chapel than church, some of which, however, are not to my credit.

The Hall, which was owned by the family who lived at the House [the Robinsons, Henry Matthew Cooper Robinson, J.P.], was usually rented to well-to-do people who could afford to keep two gardeners and three maids. My first memories of these people were of ladies who in some way were connected with Russia; they took a great interest in the children of the parish. The next tenants were a nice friendly couple who had come from Canada. The wife once told my mother that her husband had started on his way to wealth in Canada by buying a thousand sheep and selling them at once at £1 per head profit. She also prophesied on hearing of the escapades of one of my young brothers 'that boy will one day be Prime Minister, you mark my words'. A prophecy which didn't come true, alas. The next people [Charles Edward Trew was there in 1908] to occupy the Hall (I think they bought it) were a youngish couple with a family; one at least was born at the Hall. They had their personal tragedies but lived there a good many years and were well respected in the village.

It would not be too much to say that the family who lived at the House ruled the village, or thought they did. They too had had their tragedies, as the gravestones in the churchyard tell to this day, The head of the house had been simple–minded for a good many years; consequently his wife took over the mantle. She was a strong-minded and autocratic person, to say the least, and of course a fervid Tory who expected all the tenants and most of the villagers to hold the same views. Of course they were not all Tories by any means but most of them were content to keep mum about their political beliefs. My father was not one of these; although a tenant of the aforementioned lady, he didn't care if she knew he was a Liberal and as a result suffered one or two injustices at her hands. However, that is a thing of the past and best forgotten. The family at the House had a surviving daughter [Miss Cissie Robinson], who in the course of a long life did an immense amount of good in the village. It would not be too much to say that the village was life itself to her. I don't think she left it for more than a day at a time during the whole of her adult life. There will never be another like her.

The farmer families who lived in two of the nice farm houses I have already mentioned were excellent people. The younger members were good musicians and singers. They always took part in village concerts, taught at Sunday school, and trained us children in all sorts of activities. To this day I have nothing but respect for them, and many happy memories. The third big farmer was a different kettle of fish. He took little or no part in village activities, but being a 'character' his name was as much on everyone's lips as the more sober and industrious 'high-ups' or 'high moguls' as my mother used to call them. He was an auctioneer as well as a farmer, and was widely known in Norfolk. [Herbert Barcham of Knapton Old Hall] Later on I worked for him, so more about him later.

Now for some of the more pleasant episodes of village life in those days. The high light, I suppose, was the 'Parish Tea'. I think the charge for grown-ups was sixpence and for that one could feast on cold meats, sausage rolls, cakes etc. as much as one could eat. Then followed a free concert. Almost all the performers were from the village and surprisingly good they were. All took part, the people from the big houses, the tradesmen, and the working people. It was at one of these concerts that I first heard one of my favourite songs 'In the shade of the old apple tree', sung by a young man who was one of the first villagers to be killed in the Great War. In my old age I often hear this song on the radio and my thoughts go back to that crowded Parish Room with its smell of oil lamps, and the cheerful audience happily applauding.

This was not the only event of the year. There were lantern lectures, missionary meetings etc., and for the boys and girls the weekly Band of Hope meetings at which the hymn 'Yield not to temptation' was always sung. I got to hate that hymn and to this day it gives me the pip. Later on there was an organisation called the League of Mercy in which we all promised to be kind to animals. Now that was an excellent objective and probably its good effects lasted a lifetime, but the aims of the Band of Hope (anti-alcohol) were to my mind not so good. To get young children to sign the pledge and expect them to keep it all their lives was in my opinion a bit much. Still, I expect it gave the ladies of the place something to do and kept us children from mischief on Saturday afternoons.

The church choir in my younger days consisted of men and women only, but when I was about 10 or 11 a strange thing happened. A family had just moved into the parish. The son, a boy of my own age, had been a chorister in his previous church. At his first attendance at our church he walked down the aisle and sat himself down with the choir. I shall never forget the look on the face of the organist and choir-mistress (the aforementioned first lady of the village). Now this boy was undoubtedly a good singer and would be an asset to the choir, but what was to be done about it? One boy in a choir of men and women! The upshot was that all the boys and girls of the village were asked to join the choir. Quite a number agreed and that was how boys and girls first became members of the church choir. We had our choir practice separately from the adults, usually on Fridays during our dinner hour – which to me was a great bore. I didn't like being in the choir one little bit, but mother said I had to and that was that. I don't think there was a really good voice amongst the lot of us newcomers to the choir, but no doubt it was good for our souls in the long run. I am, in my old age, often accused of continually humming and singing hymns, often with the words all wrong. In fact, I had one employer who said to me one day 'Yaxley, I like to hear you whistling but I do wish you wouldn't whistle those horrible hymns'. It would have taken too long to tell her that it probably all started when that big-head of a boy forced his way into the choir; anyway it probably wouldn't have been true. All I did say was 'Well, ma'am, it might be worse, I might whistle psalms!'

Chapter 4

I ought to say that all my life I have been a bit of a lone ranger. Some pastimes necessitate a number of people taking part but on the whole I have most enjoyed those things that require no partners. Selfishness comes into this a lot I dare say and sharing things becomes a pain, especially to boys, who by and large are selfish little beasts. This applies, for instance, to cigarette card cadging, birds – nesting, gleaning, blackberrying, exploring and later on girl-chasing. I always preferred to hunt on my own.

At the time of writing this, small boys get a lot of joy zzzzing about pretending they are driving motors or tractors. In my younger days there were very few motor cars, and I never saw a tractor during my school days. Horses were the thing then. We were always riding or driving horses in our imaginations and now and again to our great joy got the chance to do these things in reality. Strangely enough, later on when I had to work with them for a time I found I was not much good with horses, they didn't seem to like me very much. At the time I was passionately fond of them and in my imagination had four magnificent horses of my own – a dapple grey, a bay, a black, and a roan. For some reason I didn't have a chestnut, it may have been because there were so few about in the days before the Suffolk Punch became so popular.

Well, in the school holidays, when I got the chance to nip off on my own I would pick up my whip (I was never without a whip), mount my chosen steed and go off for a glorious gallop along the roads and fields in search of birds' nests or blackberries, or just on exploring expeditions. My favourite horse, the grey, was a marvel. He could run and jump far better than the others, but of course I had to take them out in strict rotation.

In the birds' nesting season I roamed the countryside for miles in the evenings and weekends. My hands were a mass of scratches. Every season my mother used to warn me that I mustn't let the policeman see my hands or he would run me in. I only took one egg from each nest I found, and none at all if I'd already got two of that sort. Eggs when collected were always put in a boy's cap, the peak end, and the cap put on again. This may seem a dangerous way to transport eggs, but I never remember a sticky scalp caused by a broken egg. I had quite a good collection of egg shells, which I kept until I was in my teens. Then they all went for a burton. One of my younger brothers was ill in bed and to keep him from being too bored my mother gave him my collection of eggs to look at. It wasn't long before he crunched them into little pieces with his hands. Not one egg remained. As I have said I was in my teens at the time and had other things to occupy my mind, so the blow was not so severe as it might have been a few years earlier.

All the birds that nested in our parish I knew, but strangely enough I never saw a bullfinch until I was in my teens. My brothers found a young one and reared it in a birdcage. It lived for about nine years, and could say short words like its name (Peter) and whistle a little tune which we always called 'Look out boys here comes the copper'. Magpies and woodpeckers I had never seen until Witton Woods were cut down in the Second World War, when these birds were apparently forced out into the surrounding countryside. Little birds, which I always took to be flycatchers but which were probably not, nested in a shallow hole in a certain beech tree every year of my schooldays and for years after that, not the same pair of course but no doubt they were of the same family. I was once mystified by a nest I could see in the middle of a huge clump of brambles; it was about the size of a blackbird's nest and the outside was made entirely of a lovely green moss and looked very pretty indeed. Thinking I had found a nest built by a type of bird that was unknown to me, I decided to hack my way in. It took me hours, and when I eventually got to it I found it was only the nest of a common thrush. Thrushes usually build with dried grass and I can only think that the moss was close at hand and the thrush took advantage of it. I often used to dream I was finding beautiful eggs of birds I had never seen, just as in later years, when I played golf, I would dream I had found dozens of brand-new golf balls.

I loved blackberrying. Perhaps it was because many of the fields were clear of corn crops by the time blackberries were ripe, and the lovely late summer and autumn colours of the hedgerows could be enjoyed. Also one could clearly see the burrows and runs of the rabbits. I always longed to catch a rabbit but never could. I tried in all sorts of ways and spent many hours watching them. It was many years later, when approaching middle age, that I had a fair amount of success at that game. I think I must have picked more blackberries than any other country boy of my age. My mother was always glad to have them to help feed her growing

31

family [seven boys and one girl], and being a terrific jam maker we always had plenty of blackberry jam. If I had an extra big picking I would walk to Mundesley with a basket full and a wooden pint measure and do a bit of house-to-house selling at three ha'pence a pint, coming home as a rule with an empty basket. I didn't know Mundesley very well and now and again got confused by the rows of houses. I shall never forget the amused look on the face of one lady when she came to the back door to see me standing there: 'Why I bought some from you only ten minutes ago,' she said.

I was always keen to earn a few coppers, fetching milk, running errands etc., and usually had a bit of luck that way although I remember one year hearing my mother telling another woman that 'Alfred has only earned a penny the whole summer'. This was quite true. I got it for taking a farm worker's dinner into the harvest field for just one day. Living next door to us was an old retired fisherman who made a poor living curing herrings into bloaters, and one winter I had to go the length of The Street trying to sell these. This was before I went to school in the morning. I remember the price, penny each or two for three ha'pence. Whether I had a good sale or not I've forgotten. I don't remember ever being paid for my work, but I expect there was an arrangement between my mother and the old man. Some boys would get a harvest job 'hallorin holjer'. At that time I didn't know what 'holjer' meant, but later on I thought it could mean 'hold ye'. 'Hallorin' meant shouting or calling. When corn was being loaded into the wagons two men were loading and two men put the sheaves up to them with pitchforks. When these pitchers were ready to move the boy riding the horse had to shout 'holjer', which gave a warning to the men on the load, otherwise they might have been thrown over by the sudden jerk. I was never lucky enough to get a job like that but except for the summer of the lone penny I mostly earned something at other work.

When I was twelve years of age I tried my luck as a caddy at Mundesley golf course. The first day I earned nothing. The second day looked like being the same until after tea, when I was called to caddy for a young man with a little black moustache. I don't think I knew his name, but I shall never forget his face. To me at that time he was almost godlike – he had given me my first job as a caddy. I have handed my mother much bigger sums of money since then but none gave me so much happiness as the one and threepence I handed over then. For the rest of the summer I earned at least something every day – nothing compared with some of the older and more experienced boys, but it was a good healthy life and put into me a great love for golf. Even so I never dreamed that twenty years later I should be playing over that same course with my own clubs, and enjoying every game I played except when playing badly or losing a lot of golf-balls. Golf is one of the finest games.

Chapter 5

I have mentioned a certain farmer and auctioneer who lived in our parish. I had often worked for him at odd times during my school days. My sister and I, with a few more children, once spent a whole Saturday stone-picking in one of his fields. We each had a bucket and put the big stones in this and then into regular heaps to be carted away later. One of the farm workers picked with us and kept us in order. It was, I remember, a bitterly cold windy day and would have been very unpleasant for adults, never mind children. Our pay was to have been threepence a day. Whether the other children got their money I don't know, but I do know my sister and I didn't get ours. My parents wouldn't let us go again thank God. I have often worked for nothing since then, but nothing has ever rankled me so much as the memory of the day I went stone-picking for threepence and didn't get it.

The same farmer employed two maids in his house, but often they would be servantless and it was then I was often called upon to work in the house on a Sunday. I had to start work at 7 in the morning and my first job was to pump water up to the tanks upstairs, so many hundred strokes was the quota. The pump was in the scullery and I can recall now the cold of the pump handle on a drear winter's morning. After that job was done I had to wash up a pile of crocks and saucepans left over from the night before, clear up the grates and fireplaces in other parts of the house, light fires and carry in wood and coal.

About 8.30 or 9 o'clock the old man would come down in his dressing gown, crumble some bread in a basin, heat some milk, pour it over the bread, pop some sugar on and that was my breakfast. Shortly after, the rest of the family would come down and soon I would get the tantalising smell of bacon, sausages etc. frying in the kitchen as they cooked their breakfast. I never saw it, I was not allowed in the kitchen except when absolutely necessary. The scullery was my work place. After breakfast it was washing up, preparing vegetables and other jobs and all the time I could smell the meat cooking for dinner and other delicious smells. Naturally being a growing boy I began to look forward to my dinner. This, I must explain, was my first Sunday. About 12.30 the old man appeared again in the scullery, cut a slice or two of bread, placed with it a little pot of home-made potted meat and a dab of butter and that was my dinner. Not for me slices of the huge joints I would sometimes glimpse on their way to the dining room.

I often wonder why the old man looked after my meals, why not his wife or grown up daughters? When the meal was over I would get stuck into the washing up again and about 4 o'clock would toddle home. I never had any pay myself but I suppose they settled up with my parents. They would have had it anyway as I never spent anything I earned, except once, when I spent a penny on a bottle of so-called Cherry drink without telling my mother and felt like a criminal for weeks after.

Before I leave my schooldays perhaps I could give a few of my impressions of village life in those times. Most working people were poor enough, there is no doubt of that, farm workers wages were thirteen shillings a week and very long hours they worked too but most men and women seemed contented enough and I never remember men being out of a job for more than a few days at a time. Women did not go out to work as they do nowadays although one summer my mother walked the two miles to Mundesley to do a day's washing for someone who took in visitors, she was paid one shilling a day and her dinner.

Of course being only a boy I didn't really know what grown ups were thinking and talking about but I imagine it was round about the time I am writing about that discontent with their lot began to stir in the minds of working people especially farm workers and what we know today as 'militancy' began to show its head. The first sign of this happened when all the workers at one farm went on strike. Irishmen were brought in to take their places. [Strikes took place at Horsham St Faith's and Trunch in May 1910 when the men asked for an extra shilling a week and to finish work at 12.30 on a Saturday. This is described in George Edwards autobiography *From Crow-scaring to Westminster*. He says he addressed a meeting of over 1,000 at Knapton.]

If I remember rightly only one other place in Norfolk supported the strikers but it didn't matter much, as far as I know they all got jobs elsewhere even if it meant leaving their own village. It was at that time I first saw steam ploughs at work and very fascinating they were to watch. Even so I greatly missed the many happy hours I used to spend with the strikers and their horses.

Several old men lived in the village, whiskery old chaps who half frightened me when I was smaller. Some of the names I recall were old Dobbs, Garnham, Wright and Laycock. The last looked like a second Abraham Lincoln. How some of them existed I don't know, they were too old for work and old age pensions hadn't come into being.

My father's father died before I was born and my grandmother had to fend for herself and two younger children. She did this mainly by laundering for one or two of the big houses and I can well remember how grateful she was when the old age pension came her way. The pension was 5 shillings a week and must have seemed to many old people the greatest blessing they had ever known.

Many years later I saw a full page cartoon in an old *Punch* depicting John Bull with a huge millstone hanging from his neck. The millstone was labelled 'Old age pensions' and the caption described the millstone as the terrific burden all future Chancellors would have to bear, well as far as I can see old age pensions didn't ruin the country and I often wonder what the cartoonist would think of things today.

I mustn't forget to mention old Dan Anguish, a tall whiskery old man who used to spend a lot of time in the blacksmith's shop, so did I, mainly waiting in the hope that the blacksmith or his assistant would open a new packet of cigarettes so that I could have the card. Old Dan had fought in the Crimean War and I would hang around hoping he would talk about it, but only once in my hearing did he ever mention it, and that was to complain of the cold in that war; apparently there was a shortage of blankets.

I have often heard people refer to the age of half an egg or half a herring, this is quite true, we children often had half an egg or half a herring. Eggs and herring were cheap but even so I have often seen my mother take a knife and slide out a few coppers from the children's money box to buy bloaters. I suppose mother was one of the best of money managers. There just wasn't enough of it to go round.

In view of the fact that wages were low it may be of interest to say how we fared as regards food. I cannot say how other families lived of course, although children have a way of finding out whether their school friends have a higher or lower standard of living than their own, and I think I had a pretty good idea as to which children in the village had 'harder' and which had better food than we did. As for our family, which in my schooldays, or rather towards the end of my schooldays, consisted of Mother and Father and five children we lived plainly and always seemed to have enough to eat and I can honestly say I never went hungry and couldn't satisfy my natural hunger at home. Of course we had meat but not very much of it and I don't suppose we missed it much. Why should we when we could have those delicious Norfolk dumplings and gravy? The flavour of the meat was in the gravy. My father always grew plenty of vegetables and a good plateful of dumplings and vegetables was a meal in itself.

There always seemed to be plenty of fruit in season (except strawberries) and Mother used to make immense fruit tarts. Rhubarb tart was our favourite and when these appeared on the table our eyes would light up and we would shout in unison 'We can eat 'er', a battle cry that lasted into the days of our youth and manhood. Pea soup made from split peas was another dish we were fond of and many times in the winter we had porridge for tea. Some people might scoff at that, but I loved it, put plenty of golden syrup and milk on it and nothing was better for growing boys. Another food we had, mostly for breakfast was a concoction Mother called pepper and salt broth. It just consisted of bread broken into a basin, a dab of butter, pepper and salt and boiling water poured over it, poor stuff you say but I liked it.

I had a great uncle, a farm worker, and he had a basin of this before going to work every working day of his life. I never found out if he had a change on Sundays. Cocoa poured over broken bread was another standby and I like it to this day. 'Cocoa-sop' my mother always called it. We even had 'tea sop' at times and of course bread and milk. Milk was a penny a pint fetched from one farm or another; skim milk was often to be had from one particular farm but Mother would have none of this. Nor would she have margarine which was a comparatively new thing in those days; anyway I don't think our village shops sold it. Most housewives baked their own bread although bakers' carts did come into the village, but baker's bread was a little bit of a luxury. We children liked it very much for a change, but really what could be nicer than little loaves of home-made bread hot from the oven, split in half and a wedge of that 'Red American' cheese stuffed in the middle, a meal fit for a king. I could go on about the subject of food, but I won't. However, I would like to mention one little incident that happened in my very young days. An older boy than me used to come and play with me; he lived up the road a few yards with his grandmother. One day his grandmother called him home to dinner, he went, but to my mother's astonishment he was back again in a few minutes. 'Why Fred,' said my mother, 'you've never had your dinner already?' 'No,' said Fred, 'I wunt hev any. What do you think she give me? A bit o' black meat with some whiskers on.' Mother was puzzled as to what this was but with a woman's natural aptitude for fying she soon found out that the 'bit o' black meat with some whiskers on' was pig's ear. We had some curious eatables in our house at times but never pig's ear thank goodness.

QUEENIE BANE (WILD)
at Knapton School from 1922 to 1930

I started school at 5 years old and left at the age of 14. The teachers I can remember were Miss Carpenter, Miss Everett, Mrs Tyrell, Mrs Cox, and Miss Doughty who was an infant teacher. I can remember doing sewing and knitting, making aprons and dolls' clothes, doing country dancing, and going on nature walks. We had garden plots at the back of the school house, I shared mine with Nina Plant (née Swan). I used to like playing netball, my favourite lesson was nature study. I used to go to Mundesley School for cookery lessons by horse and cart. The boys did carpentry. I can remember a school inspector, doctor, nit nurse, and a dentist. We had milk sometimes.

I did stencilling and made Christmas decorations. I walked to school from the bottom of Knapton Street, it took about 15 minutes.

I attended Church Sunday School. The teachers were Miss Leather and Miss Pain, and I sang in the church choir. Later, I belonged to the W.I.

The shops were run by the Watts family and Mrs Webster at the bottom of the street.

Mother cooked in a wall oven and on an open fire. She did the washing in the copper. We had a bucket toilet up the garden, water out of a well.

I considered a cockerel for dinner was a real treat. We had a garden where we kept rabbits, ferrets, chickens, and a dog. I used to help with washing up and spring cleaning, in the garden, and collecting rabbit food. I can remember food rationing and it was very poor.

I remember fêtes at Knapton House and Church Farm, and May Days on the lawn opposite Knapton Hall, dancing round the May Pole and scrambling for sweets and fruit.

I remember the outbreak of the Second World War and the end, the death of King George VI, food rationing, the snow in 1947 which cut us off completely, and the floods of 1953.

I can remember steam threshing at Wallage's White House Farm. I can also remember Burtons delivering bread, Mr Wegg from Trunch with meat, and Mr Tribbett with coal on horse and cart, and Twiggs with milk.

DOROTHY WILD (MADELEY)
at Knapton School 1925 to 1934

I remember my first day at Knapton School in the little room. Miss Tyrell was the teacher, and I remember blue birds on the walls.

I remember the cloakroom and having to cross the playground to the archáic toilets, weather conditions did not always help.

Going up to the Big Room was a thrill. My memory fails me as to the teacher there, but she was nice. I felt most important in the other part of the Big Room. The fireplace was the focal point, and the big board, and sitting on chairs with proper desks, lovely.

I did enjoy the Friday afternoons dancing to the gramophone. I also enjoyed the PE, but couldn't understand why it had to be done. 'You will know later in life', they said, and they were right. However, one very cold freezing morning our teacher of the time was Miss Thane, and she slipped full length on a slide. She did not appreciate that but we did.

The vicar used to visit and give talks, and Miss Robinson, a local important lady, and other ladies did frequently visit.

Miss Everett was the head teacher during the last year or so. I remember when Mrs Johnson arrived, she was nice and sporty.

It is fair to say that I did enjoy needlework and we had the chance to exhibit our work at various places including Norwich. This speaks well of the period, as my favourite occupations are still cross stitch and embroidery.

I did not like the dentist's visits in the van in the playground. He always smoked, ugh!

I remember many things connected with Knapton School and the village, like the village shop where we got excited when a new delivery of sugar mice arrived.

I have been very lucky to survive war time air raids, and wartime conditions nursing in Norwich, Overstrand, and for a time, North Walsham. I recall the bombing of Norwich and Overstrand, where my bedroom was hit. When the Queen presented me with my M.B.E. I admit my thoughts went to my humble beginnings, yes I honestly did.

I feel I have been further educated in the college of life. I was married in 1941 to Trevor who was a baker and confectioner in Mildenhall. I met him when he was with the Suffolk Regiment in North Norfolk. Later he was with the Royal Norfolk Regiment. When he died in 1972 I carried on the business in Mildenhall the best I could. He was heavily involved in local government and politics, which I continued for 27 years

(District and County). My three children have always supported me and we are a close family. I am proud of them, Julie, Mary and Noel.

My second husband was John Madeley, primary head teacher in Mildenhall. He died in 2004.

My 11 great grandchildren are the recipients of my hand-worked birth samplers, so you see, the lessons in needlework at Knapton paid off!

~~☙❦❧~~

ELLEN MAY DIXON (Nellie) (KIRK)
at Knapton School 1928 to 1934 (died 2007)

Attended Trunch School until the age of 8 then transferred to Knapton, walked to school leaving home at 8 a.m. and it took about 45 minutes. Having three younger sisters they eventually had one bike to share and they had a set distance and then they would ride and leave it in the hedge for the next one's turn. Sometimes they hitched a ride on the back of the milkman's cart as he was taking his milk delivery which made him very annoyed. Being the oldest she always had the new clothes and Wellington boots but by the time they were handed down to the fourth one the boots often leaked. They had to walk in all weathers and often got very wet and cold. During the year they had to spend 2 weeks at Mundesley School (now the library) for cookery and another 2 weeks doing laundry. In the cookery class they had a Miss Evans who was just out of training and they used to be very mischievous. On one occasion a girl tossed her pancake and landed it on the old cooking range, the penalty being that she had to scrape and clean it off again. At this time the boys went down to Mundesley and did woodwork.

She moved to 1 School Close in 1951 and soon after Mrs Watts, the school cleaner, became ill and too old to continue the hard work involved in the cleaning duties. After doing it on a temporary basis she took it on herself. Wintertime the work was very hard, she got up at 6 a.m. to clean out and light the fires. The Little Room had a round combustion fire and the Big Room had an open fire. She returned at 8 a.m. to bank up the fires so that it would be warm when the children arrived at 9 a.m. After school closed in the afternoon she would go in between 4 p.m. and 5 p.m., sweep classrooms and porches and clean sinks and outside toilets (these were 'bucket and chuck-its' and emptied by Joe Bane twice a week).Toilet seats were wood and needed scrubbing regularly. Before she left she would get in heavy buckets of coal ready for the following morning. What a relief when summertime came and no fires to do.

During the Summer Holidays she would have to give everything a special clean. All the floors were wooden floorboards and had to be scrubbed while on hands and knees. After a year of school children on them in wet days and all the dirty painting etc. it was quite a hard and dirty task.

Miss Townsend was responsible for the kitchen although the dinners were cooked at Bacton School and brought over in aluminium containers by David or John Pell. Nellie took over dinner lady duties in the 1950s. She helped to put up the dinner tables and benches for the infants. The juniors had special wipe-clean covers and had their dinner on their desks. She laid out the cutlery and helped dish out the dinners. After the food she went out on playground duty until classes started again at 1.15. This part of the job she really loved as she adored children and they all seemed to like her. She was quite strict but very fair. In the early years they played in the playground and she spent hours turning a big skipping rope and keeping order when 'What's the time Mr Wolf' was being played. Later after the purchase of the playing field they were able to spread their wings a little more, playing football and going on the swings. While the money was being raised for the playing field she contributed a lot of her time to fundraising, helping with whist drives, Christmas sales etc. cooking cakes and making gifts to be sold for funds.

As a school helper she was asked to accompany the children on school trips.

In June the children went on a trip to London. They caught the train at Knapton station, changing at Norwich and arriving at Liverpool St.

An early picture of Knapton Station. The church can be seen in the background.

Visits included Buckingham Palace, The Tower of London and the Crown Jewels, Natural History Museum, Science Museum, The Royal Tournament. On one occasion one boy did not get off the underground train and they saw the train leave with him still on board. A quick phone-call to the next station and a member of the underground staff got him off and put him on the next train back, what an adventure for a country boy, and a panic for the staff and helpers until his safe return to them. On another occasion a best coat was left on the underground train never to be seen again.

In July the juniors went on a day trip to Blakeney Point. A coach took them to Morston Quay. They walked out to the Point over the marshes and came back by boat after digging for cockles, and seeing the seals and terns.

Also in July the infants used to have a coach to Cromer and spend a day on the beach. Often lunch was in the shelters due to the cold weather and to avoid sand in the sandwiches.

In October/November a trip was organized to Yarmouth to see the Scottish herring fishing fleet.

Nellie really enjoyed her time with the children at Knapton School and was very sad the day it closed as the heart of the community had been taken away.

ROY FAWKES
at Knapton School 1934 to 1946

The Big Room had 2 classes, 8 to 11 years and 11 to 14 years, the Little Room was for the infants (4 to 8 years).

It was freezing cold in the winter and very hot in the summer.

There was no kitchen in those days, 2 of us boys each shared a garden to grow vegetables and the girls had a flower garden and lawn.

An Infant teacher (I think her name was Miss Walwark) who came from North Walsham, a nasty, spiteful, cruel teacher. One Friday afternoon she just left the classroom, she didn't wait for the end of the class, just after lunch she packed her bag and left. I think she thought that she would get a rough send off from the children and parents. We kids were left in the room on our own. Mrs Johnson came to see what all the noise was and found we were alone and so sent one of the older girls in to look after us.

After Miss Walwark came Daisy Willow, she was a lovely teacher, then after her was Miss Doughty.

1935/6

One day we were taken out into the playground to see a great big airship flying over.

We had a big party on the lawn at Knapton Hall to celebrate King George V's silver jubilee.

We had a big old gramophone and we used to carry it out into the playground for dancing.

1939

Evacuees came to the village late 1939. They came from Hackney in the east end of London. We had 2 boys staying with us, Bill was 10 and George was 8. They stayed until late 1940 when it was thought that the Germans might invade East Anglia.

While the evacuees were here the school was not big enough so the village children had the school in the morning and the evacuees used the village hall and then everyone swapped round at lunchtime.

1943

The Americans were here in the Air Force and on Thanksgiving Day one of the officers came to talk to us about America and the schools back there. He also brought lots of chocolates and sweets.

1944

On D-Day June 6th Mrs Johnson brought in her radio so that we could all hear Winston Churchill's broadcast of the invasion of Europe from the House of Commons.

Other memories

School dinners started when Mrs Johnson asked the children who walked from Swafield and Trunch to bring in a potato each to bake on the open fire in the big room, so that they had something to eat at midday.

Then she started cooking on oil stoves with steamers and ovens for a few pence a day.

Then the older girls cooked the dinners as part of cookery lessons.

In the end any of the children could stay (not just those that walked in every morning from the other villages). All the cooking was done in the classroom during the lessons, the boys had to put covers over the desks at lunchtime and then had to wash-up afterwards.

We used to walk to school, the school milk was warmed in front of the fire in the Big Room, it was 1/2d a bottle.

One of the school outings was a trip to St Andrew's Hall in Norwich for a singing festival.

A Knapton School outing to a singing festival in Norwich.
The three teachers are Mrs Johnson, Mrs Burrel and Miss Doughty.

In 1946 all the children that had left school the previous year were invited back to go on a school outing for the first trip after the war. It was to London and London Zoo. It cost about 10 shillings to go on the trip.

Electricity came to the village in about 1946.

Running water came in about 1958.

Mains sewerage still waiting!

We had a garden and allotment; we kept rabbits, pigs, goats and dogs. We had to gather food from the hedgerows to feed the rabbits.

All the shopping was done in North Walsham.

We had ration books for everything, food, sweets and clothing.

Sports days were held in the meadow opposite the hall, this is now where the housing estate is. This was Mr Dixon's Field where he usually kept his cows. This meant that when we had a race we had to race up and down the field avoiding the cow pats!

I had bananas and oranges before the war.

JOY LEE
at Knapton School 1935 to 1944

Joy remembers Miss Walwark in the Infants Class. At the start of her schooling slates *and* chalk were used as there were no books. But books more in use after Joy progressed to The Big Room. Joy can remember the School Nurse looking for lice in heads. Joy also recalls how the older girls would do the cooking for lunches, supervised by Mrs Johnson, before the kitchen was built. She says 'We made wonderful chocolate steamed pudding and custard'. And it was all cooked on oil burners and in steamers. Joy remembers that before the school had a piano there was an organ where mice happily nested. Mr Coe from The Station House bought the organ and Joy remembers seeing it there when she went to tea with her friend Dot Coe.

Joy recalls enormous fun putting on a puppet show, 'A Christmas Carol'. It was shown at Knapton, Trunch and Mundesley. Mr Mallett who kept Trunch Post Office made all the puppets and Joy's puppet was Scrooge.

Joy also remembers sewing lessons and making a dress. It was all hand sewn and a tremendous achievement. She also remembers knitting a pair of socks on four needles. Joy remembers milk being warmed on the hearth in front of the fire in cold weather. She also recalls growing vegetables in the school garden and Evelyn Ashley and she won first prize, beating the boys.

Like most other children Joy walked to school and it took about 10 to 15 minutes to get there. During the war years when evacuees came to the village Joy remembers half days at school. She remembers gathering waste paper and acorns which was all stored at Wallages Farm till it was collected for recycling.

School concerts were a regular feature and Joy recalls dressing as a milkmaid and singing 'Where are you going to my pretty maid?' with Sammy Miffen. At the outbreak of World War II Joy was in church and Reverend Prichard announced war had been declared. Joy remembers Miss Watts in the Post Office before Mrs Smith taking it over.

Miss Montford took Sunday school at this time. Joy belonged to the Chapel Youth Group who met at Raxawa in Mundesley. This was a large house which the Chapel used for conferences and for youth ventures. Here you could play billiards, tennis, and badminton and meet other young people of your age.

Joy also sang in the church choir and remembers village fêtes where children danced with hoops and did country dancing. Bowling for the pig was a very popular sideshow. Joy remembers the snows of 1947 when Mundesley road was blocked and she had to walk over the fields to work.

She remembers steam threshing at Wallages Farm and notes she preferred to watch when it was done by horse power.

Joy recalls Eric Pardon passing The Scholarship and how everyone was delighted with his success. He was the first to pass from Knapton School.

On the home front Joy remembers Sunday tea as a treat when they had peaches and cake. Joy also remembers keeping rabbits, chickens and two pigs at home and collecting rabbit food and cleaning the hutches, She remembers having an iced lolly from a Walls Ice Cream cart that was pedal powered. The advert on the cart read 'Stop me and buy one'.

Fetching water was a regular chore from the pump about four houses down the road. When the pump was out of order it was further to walk to the well and she recalls the bucket being so big it took two to pull it up.

Joy now lives in Werrington near Peterborough with her husband Basil and has a daughter, Karen, and a grandson, James.

LLEWELLYN KIRK
at Knapton School 1935 to 1941

The shops in Knapton were all on the left side of The Street. Miss Watts', which was the first one going down the Street, was a General Stores. Jill Watts' parents lived on the other side of the Street. Their garden was on the other side of the track which led down to the field beside their bungalow. Lou Watts called it the pightle.

The second shop was run by Grace Wright. That was a General Stores, and was set back from the road, opposite the entrance to Billy Small's carpenter's shop. The third was Smith's Post Office and General Store down the bottom of the Street.

My father was in the 5th Battalion TA Norfolk Regiment, Robert Kirk. I was with him, when he worked for Geaves in Mundesley. We were in the harvest field, and a dispatch rider came and told him he had been called up, two weeks before war was declared.

The Battalion moved to Weybourne. They thought the Germans would invade there, there being no cliffs there. They shot a plane down and it contained maps and photos of all the trenches and gun emplacements in the area. So that was what the airship had been doing over Norfolk! So they all had to be changed.

After a while, he was transferred to the 1st Battalion as a Sergeant. He was lucky as the 5th got taken in Singapore. He was sent to Chelsea Barracks in London with the Guards. They got bombed badly and his nerves went. After being in Shenley Hospital, he was discharged from the Army or any other military service.

He worked for Miss Robinson for a while. Then he joined the Home Guard and got made up to Second Lieutenant. I used to go around with them as Chief Scout. Other villages used to be the enemy, so I used to hide in the hedge and run back and tell the Knapton crowd that they were coming.

We left Norfolk in April 1945 to go to Wales. We had a Pickford container to take the furniture by rail, £17. 10s. My mother, who was Welsh, wanted to go home, for her Welsh chapel etc. My father had various jobs down there, civilian batman to the Commanding Officer at St Athens Airfield, and he also worked for the Steel Company of Wales. I started a five year apprenticeship as coachbuilder and wheelwright. I was a month too late to go to technical college, so I had to start work at fourteen years old. I finished my apprenticeship and did two years in the Army, and then three and a half years in the T.A. Welsh Regiment.

I got married in 1959. We had two children. The reason we moved to Cambridge was that my daughter got bad asthma and the doctors advised us to move from the Valleys because of the weather.

My mother died in 1982. So we moved my father to Waterbeach in sheltered accommodation. My daughter died in 1985. My father died in Addenbrooke's three months later. He couldn't understand why our daughter had to die at 24 years old and him 80.

ROGER DIXON
at Knapton School 1939 to 1945

One of my first memories of Knapton School is of reading with Miss Doughty. I came upon the word 'ashamed', which I read as ash a med, and she found it hard to convince me that the second 'a' made a different sound from the first. One occasion when I really was ashamed took place later, when I was in the 'big room'. We were out gardening and Mrs Johnson sent me back to the tool shed to fetch a rake. Some older boys were there (I can't remember now who they were) and they wouldn't let me have it. I was there long enough for Mrs Johnson to come herself to see where I was. She arrived at the moment when I said that I must have it, 'Kitty wants it!' I was sent into the school, and much later when all the others had gone home and I was still there, Mrs Watts arrived and said that she was surprised at me. I think they were secretly amused, but didn't let on. Years later, when I mentioned it to Mrs Watts, she had, of course, forgotten all about it.

There was a little room opposite the door into the infant room which was used in my time as a store. I used to think that it was a mysterious place. A favourite piece of furniture was in the corner of the big room. It was where stationery supplies were kept. I loved the smell.

One year we entered a singing competition at St Andrew's Hall in Norwich. There is a photograph of the whole school assembled in the cloisters there. A lady called Miss Burrell came from Bacton to train and conduct us. She struck me as a very formidable lady and, even if we had been inclined, she wouldn't have stood any nonsense. I seem to remember a song 'I met an engine on the road'. That's something you don't see any more! By the way, I can't remember whether or not we won. I should hardly think so considering the bigger schools which must have been in the competition.

I was in her class when Miss Doughty suddenly became Mrs Woodage. I suspect that the match was a great surprise to everyone, even Mrs Johnson. As to the other teachers, I knew Miss Collier only through meeting her as we cycled to school, she to Knapton, I with Eric Pardon, to North Walsham. She used to sweep round the corner of Bacton Road at North Walsham in a great circle. I believe that is where she had a bad accident. In those days no-one knew who had the right of way. She would be within the law today. I have come across Mr and Mrs Featherstone through the Methodist Church, at Fakenham and, of course, at North Walsham.

My favourite lessons were what we would today call geography. Some of them came from a radio programme about an imaginary village called Dylsford. I already had a great love of maps from my father, but this taught us about contours, OS symbols and about the social life of a village. To this day, I can get a great deal of pleasure just reading a map. Mrs Johnson did some inspired work on our own village. I remember learning about its acreage, its farms, about the transfer of Knapton Cottage and its area to Mundesley, and so on. And that brings me to say how fortunate we all were. As someone who went first into teaching, I know that we were taught by someone who was years before her time. Those of us who went on to higher education owe everything to her.

One area where she had less success with me was in maths. Poor Miss Doughty was getting nowhere in the little room with my sums, and then along came a teacher evacuated from London, a Jewish lady called Miss Cohen. She managed to get through to me and I began to understand. Mrs Johnson had something to go on, but I was still pretty thick! While I'm on this paragraph, others will remember how we used to use the school alternate days with the evacuees. We would be in the school one day and the Parish Room (as we called it then) the next. If we were kept separate, how I came to be taught by Miss Cohen, I can't remember.

There are so many other things. Singing together was another pleasure. All the nature studies were enjoyed. I remember finding an old nest of some yellowhammers with Reggie Smith and bringing it for display. A lot of these studies followed a pattern from a magazine Mrs Johnson took and were written by Enid Blyton. I loved the readings we had from her books, too.

I was always a bookish sort of boy and used to get a bit of teasing, especially on the way home. So it wasn't unalloyed happiness. Perhaps for that reason, apart from Reggie who kindly put up with me, my closest friend was Llewellyn Kirk, who lived near us in the Street, but went to school at Mundesley. I think it was probably the best time in the whole history of the school, and all because of one person.

A Wartime Childhood

Everyone understands that the war loomed large in the lives of those who served in the forces and in the struggles of mothers to feed their families in a time of rationing. But it also played an enormous part in the lives of children. One thing which I always remember is the visits of American airmen to Knapton School. They brought gifts of 'candy' and we, in turn were taught the American national anthem, 'Oh! Say do you see, by the dawn's early light?' I don't know where they came from – which base, I mean – but we certainly enjoyed their visits. Apart from the land mine which came down in one of Mr May's fields and damaged his Mundesley road barn and blew out some glass in the windows of the church, Knapton came through unscathed. But I remember standing at my bedroom window which looked south and seeing the sky red from the fires in Yarmouth during the big incendiary raids on the harbour and town. I had an operation on my right foot during the war and went to Norwich on the train for a check-up at the hospital. My mother and I had to pick our way up St Stephen's over the ruins of an air raid. There were police and wardens helping and directing people. Because men were called up and sometimes posted to distant places, there were also some weddings quickly celebrated before they went. Miss Doughty's sudden appearance at school as Mrs Woodage, is an example. I've got a photograph of Miss Josephine Kiernan's wedding to Jack Ringer. My uncles and aunts are on it because some of them worked for the Kiernans, but otherwise it is a lovely record of the great and the good of wartime Knapton society.

While the Kiernan family are in mind, I recall another incident involving them. My mother used to go one afternoon a week to do the washing in their laundry. I always joined her after school. One day I was singing as I played in the garden and Mrs Kiernan, who had been, I think, an opera singer, heard me and called down from her window, 'Who's that singing?' I hid in the shrubbery, but it transpired that she wasn't cross, but simply interested. She offered to give me singing lessons and train my voice, but soon after that she became more frail and nothing came of it. I often wonder what might have been.

Singing and music played a big part in the life of our family – that is, in the Gee family, my grandmother's people. Every Christmas we had an enormous party crammed into the cottage where Walter Pardon, the last of the folk singers lived. He was the last of the family to live there, where they had been since the 1830s. There was a big beam across the middle of what was then the 'front room' and the entertainment swung from one side of it to the other. After a song, or an item on an instrument (several of them played, violin, accordion, flute) suitable refreshment followed and then there was a call of 'Your side o' the baulk!' and a person on that side of the room would oblige. In later years, after Peter Bellamy, whom I taught at Fakenham Grammar School, 'discovered' Walter, one of Walter's records was given that title. He kept the big drum of the Knapton band in his shed, and there were all sorts of family tales about music-making in the past. One was that the family formed the church band in the reign of William IV in the 1830s, before the Robinson family provided the first harmonium. If you have ever read Thomas Hardy's *Under the Greenwood Tree* you will know how the Gees felt about it.

That brings me to the Church. I absolutely loved church as a boy. It was like being at a beautiful play, performed every week, mostly the same, but with fascinating changes as the seasons came round. Mr Prichard, the Rector at the time, was a wonderful visitor to my father, who had quite serious heart trouble. He called one day, chuckling to himself. He had visited Mr Wallage, at White House Farm and had asked whether he thought we should pray for rain. He got the answer, 'What's the good of that with the wind where it is?' I think Mr Wallage

Miss Josephine Kearnan's wedding group at Knapton Old Hall in 1941

Mrs Johnson is standing 6th from the left, Miss Montford standing 9th from the left. Mr and Mrs Norman May are standing at the back 1st and 2nd from the right, Miss Robinson 5th from the right. Kathleen Johnson is in the front row 1st on left.

may have been having him on, but he was greatly amused. One thing I remember about Christmas time is that Mr Prichard would not allow carols to be sung until Christmas actually came, unlike today, when we sing them all through December.

Sunday School was run by Miss Montford, who had a great enthusiasm for the Melanesian Mission to the South Sea Islands. A whist table was always arranged like a little altar, with a cross and flowers. The child whose birthday fell that week took home the flowers. I, or perhaps my mother, lost out because my birthday is in late December. As a teenager I started going to the Christian Endeavour at the Chapel, but my mother and father, strongly Anglican, didn't really approve. Happily those days have gone and in my later life I have had wonderfully happy times with the Salvation Army, the Methodist and Baptist Churches and even the Brethren, though they didn't invite me any more after I was ordained.

We lived when I was very small in a bungalow where Stanley Dixon's house stands today. But we moved up the street to what is now 'Autumn Cottage' when I was about five. At both places we were neighbours of Mrs Adeline Watts, and she played a significant part in my childhood. So did her husband, because it is from him that I learnt my first swear words! We shared the same well and as I got older, I used to draw water for her. I also dug enormous holes in her field at the back for waste - and I mean enormous. They were about six feet square and I needed a ladder to get out. Georgie Hewitt was always on hand to help. Adeline was terrified of thunder and I sometimes got up in the middle of the night to go down to her and Georgie. In the summer I occasionally went to tea there and I remember we always had the same thing, tomatoes from Mr Loveday, and cheese from the shop. Adeline had been a wonderful cook, as I recall, but in later years she gave up the oven entirely. I can remember the outbreak of war and heard the Prime Minister's announcement on her wireless.

When electricity came to the village I was at the Grammar School, and I remember hoping every afternoon as I biked home, that they would have got to us, and we should be connected when I got there. 'Three lights and a plug', I think it was, and anything after that you had to pay.

Until then many of us had our wireless batteries charged by Mr Bridges at Mundesley. It was a great nuisance when they ran out just before a good evening's listening. There was still local entertainment even during the war, particularly events to raise money in the various weeks decreed by the government for the war effort. There were concerts in the Parish Room, Barn Dances in Mr May's barn and other similar things. I can't remember exactly when it was, but a production of Shakespeare's *A Midsummer Night's Dream* was put on at the Old Hall. It was in the open air, under an enormous beech tree. A girl called Dorothy Green and I were in it – as bumble-bees. I think the casting may have been due to our shape! Mr Twigg from the Dairy at Mundesley was one of the players. He had a quick draw on his pipe in the bushes 'backstage', but was called for the next scene and stuffed the pipe into his pocket. Part-way through the scene his jacket began to smoulder and a thin spiral of smoke began to rise. I was very young at the time and I don't remember much about the other actors, but they were all local people. Mr Claydon (Arthur's father) was one and my uncles George and Hubert. They were Bottom the weaver and the other 'mechanicals'. As to the serious characters, the big parts, I have no memories at all. It was the funny ones I liked.

The Kiernan family also produced a Nativity play and there is a photograph of the cast. I don't remember much about it, except the star which my uncle Hubert contrived out of a bicycle lamp which was pulled on a cord across the stage to rest 'above where the young child was'. The adult cast have all long since gone, but Arthur Claydon who was an angel is the only survivor I know. We have all become so used to slick TV films and shows in our own homes so I suppose we would think these countrified productions very tame, but they were much enjoyed at the time.

Mrs Johnson made sure that our horizons were widened by our annual school trips to London. These were after the war, of course, but they were very exciting to us as children. There was one occasion when John Rayner and I didn't get off the tube in time and the doors closed on us. We got off at the next stop, crossed over and returned. Mrs Johnson was very pleased with us and the search which London Transport (if that is what it was called at the time) had just begun was called off. Few of us had travelled out of Norfolk in the war years and the journeys to and from London were nearly as exciting as the destination itself.

Sometimes we really were confined to Knapton. The heavy snow in the winter of 1947 cut the village off from the outside world and a train was stuck in a huge drift between Knapton and Mundesley. Several people have photographs of the drifts, particularly in Hall Lane, and of the men who dug their way through. There was one drift I specially remember, right over the kissing gate at the top of the path across the Well Piece to the station. The snow began to melt and then froze again, leaving a crust. You could walk right over the gate and the hedge.

It was a great loss when the railway closed, but the thinking about national transport was different fifty years ago. Writing 'fifty years' reminds me that I had left Knapton by then. The branch was not a very long-lasting one. In fact it opened and closed in my father's lifetime. He had a free ride with the other Knapton children on the first train and he also travelled on the last. It's not all loss, however. The cutting in Hall Lane and the Paston Way running along the old track are a real amenity. The station may have been a good walk from parts of the village. So were the buses for many of us. But nobody minded a walk or a bike ride in those days.

The railway provided a walk for some of us even then and I remember going on it where it runs along Water Lane (now grown up and blocked) and near Pigness Farm. The wood now called Pigney's Wood is on the land of that farm, and it was spelt Pigness in those days. The Dewing family moved out of the house and it was ruined in the war, being used by soldiers stationed at Swafield Hall for battle training. Edward Langham (evacuated with his sister Josephine to Mr and Mrs Johnson) and I found thunder flashes there.

Some others may remember military manoeuvres in the village. One night there was scuffling outside and my parents went to investigate. A soldier made desperate signs not to have his hiding place in our currant bushes betrayed. The shrubbery of the Hall gardens, opposite where we lived, was another hiding place. In those days nightingales came there in the summer. Now, of course, it is built on – St Peter's Close. I'm not sure about that address. On the one hand it may be seen as a comfort, on the other, I want to avoid meeting the apostle for as long as I can.

I remember Mundesley Garage (now Jen-Bar) being burnt down during the war. It was an accidental fire, nothing to do with the war itself. My father went in to try to rescue the hire car and only just escaped, as the roll-over door came down in front of him, the fire taking his eyebrows and the front of his hair. They moved to a Dutch barn in a field belonging to Mr Geaves at the Rookery at Mundesley. He was sworn to secrecy, so we did not know at the time, but it came out afterwards that they were doing work on searchlights.

My father worked at Mundesley Garage until his first heart attack, and after that, though never fully fit. I used to go and meet him because my mother was worried about him biking up the long drawn-out hill from Mundesley. There followed a long period when he could not work, and some of the lighter jobs that were offered by the Labour Exchange were quite impossible. One was operating a ride at the Pleasure Beach at Yarmouth. How was he to get there? My Uncle George who took over the holding from my great uncle Alfred (Dan Dixon) was very kind to us. At one stage the only decent jacket I had was my school blazer. There was a Mission from the Cambridge University Christian Union and my mother and I went to a meeting on the Green round the bus shelter. As we approached, I overheard one young man say to another, 'Here come the village intelligentsia!' I was mortified, and have always had a mistrust of that kind of aggressive Christianity ever since. It made me a high churchman.

Another of my mother's many jobs was as caretaker of what we then called the Parish Room. I used to help clear up after whist drives, and other functions. As I look back I recognise what a hard life she had and am truly grateful. They gave up a lot for me and her early death made it impossible to show all that gratitude. I have recently discovered that my last year at the Grammar School, beyond my A levels, as I tried for Cambridge, was paid for by two of the governors. My parents could not have met the costs, and I have gone all through life wondering how it happened.

I am starting to realise that this is less about Knapton and more about me! But it is the story of someone who looks back with a certain kind of longing to those days. There were very few cars about in the war, and people would stop and ask where you were going and if you wanted a lift. Neighbours, like Adeline, meant so much more. The social life of families and of the village was much more lively. I wonder how many others remember the mobile cinema that used to come and set up a screen in the driveway of the Hall, sheltered, and, I suppose, darkened by the trees, and show mostly Ministry of Information films. It is easy when you are old to look back and see all these things through rose-tinted spectacles, but they were happy though hard times. It is ironic that there isn't a word in English to describe the feeling that comes over me these days, but that the Welsh, among whom I now live, do have such a word. It is 'hiraeth' and it means longing, with touches of nostalgia, home-sickness, and even grief, thrown in. And that's how I feel as I look back on my Knapton childhood.

DAVID LEE
at Knapton School 1941 to 1947

David remembers that during the war years the children were given two weeks off for fruit picking. You had to get a card signed to prove you had been, and he remembers skiving off by getting his card signed at the start of the day rather than at the end! He remembers Miss Walwark as his teacher in the Infants class as cruel and nasty and that children would rather wet their pants than ask her if they could go to the lavatory. He remembers Mrs Johnson as a star who was a very good teacher. David remembers school plays in the Parish Rooms and also having First Aid lessons with Mr Mallett of Trunch Post Office.

David collected acorns and waste paper like everyone else and remembers land girls and prisoners of war on Cargill's farm. He also remembers stealing some bread and cheese from home to give to a German PoW whom he felt very sorry for. As his big brother was in the army, David worried what he would say when he was found out. It seems Jimmy wished the bloke Good Luck. David had his own little plot in the School garden and won a prize for best radishes. David remembers Roger Dixon, Reggie Smith, Dick Eastoe, Nancy Miller and Pongo Bayes and Bob Pearman, who was the champion for anyone being bullied.

David now lives with his wife, Hazel, in Ditchingham, Bungay. David has a son, Christopher and two daughters, Pippa and Debbie. He has a grand daughter, Rowan.

⁓≈ஜ୨୧ஜ≈⁓

ANN LEE (ISITT)
at Knapton School 1941 to 1947

Knapton, sixty years ago was a small village with a school, church and post office with General Stores. There was also a Blacksmith, but today only the church remains. When I was a little girl, Mrs Smith kept the Post Office right down the bottom of the street, past the church and past the farm, on the left before you took the road under the bridge to Paston. Later on, the Post Office moved up the road, still on the left and just past the church, and was run by Mrs Dixon and Miss Townsend. When that closed, Knapton lost its own little shop. My elder sister, Daphne remembers the Post Office being at the cross roads where there is still a posting box, and this shop was run by a Miss Adams. In those days we knew everyone who lived in the village, and the priest, teacher and policeman were highly respected. So too were Miss Robinson and Miss Leather who lived at Knapton House and who were key figures in village life. They were the 'gentry'. Miss Robinson played the church organ and held weekly choir practices. She also started a club for us in The Parish Rooms where we had Beetle Drives and played board games. Miss Leather took Sunday School and I remember each year on Mothering Sunday she gave each child a posy of beautifully tied violets for their mothers. We were rather in awe of these ladies but they were very kind and when I was ill with whooping cough and pneumonia, Miss Robinson called to our house with good things to help me get better. Calves foot jelly was something I remember well and have never tasted since all those years ago!

I remember too, Mr Bussey, the Blacksmith, who had his forge opposite the Loke that was the short cut to the railway station. Yes, trains ran from Knapton until Mr Beeching axed dozens of local lines in the sixties. Mr Bussey had an orchard in the Loke, and some very succulent Victoria plums were top favourites to try and scoop up along with a few apples, before an irate Mr B. gave chase. The smell of the sulphur, the clang of the iron and the red hot heat are vivid memories as we stood and watched the farm horses being shod.

Now, after sixty odd years I probably would only recognize half a dozen people in Knapton at the most. Of course a lot of my mother's contemporaries are dead, and my peers, like me, moved away in the 1950s. But Norfolk has a great attraction with those huge expansive skies and I came 'home' when I retired in 1996. From 1932 Mrs Kitty Johnson was the Headmistress and she had a tremendous influence on our young lives. From the age of five in 1941 I was a pupil along with my brother David and little sister, Yvonne. All our family attended Knapton School and all remember Mrs Johnson with great affection. I was one of the lucky ones and at the age of eleven went on to North Walsham High School (now part of Paston Sixth Form College) having passed the 11+ or The Scholarship as it was referred to in those days.

Mrs Johnson was an incredible woman. About 40 children (sometimes less) attended the school between the ages of 5 and 14 years in two rooms with two teachers, somehow teaching all age groups with remarkable success. Certainly we all knew our tables and were both literate and numerate on leaving school. I recall Mrs Johnson having three or four children round the blackboard to explain the intricacies of some mathematical problems, then that group sitting down to continue work on an exercise based round the lesson whilst another two or three gathered at the blackboard for their lesson.

Painting, Nature Study, P.E. Country Dancing and Singing were all on the curriculum. Knitting and Embroidery was often going on quietly while individual children stood at Mrs Johnson's desk to read to her or have homework corrected.

There are so many memories. I well remember learning to knit on four needles and how to turn a heel on a sock. I recall Nature walks, collecting wild flowers to press and name on our return to school. Green

Lane, by the Railway Station was a marvellous hunting ground where we discovered owl pellets, abandoned birds' eggs, and at the right time of year, a glut of blackberries for pies. We also collected hips and haws in the war years as a source of vitamin C. Wallages Pit gave us frog-spawn to study and watch the tadpoles turn into frogs. And of course we kept caterpillars and learned the wonder of metamorphosis.

Who ever could forget Country Dancing? The wonderful gramophone complete with trumpet horn and Mrs Johnson leaping to crank the handle as the record speed slowed down as we whirled around enjoying Strip the Willow, Gathering Peascods and The Gay Gordons. Marvellous fun, leaving us all exhausted at the end of the lesson.

Everyone worked hard during the war and even if you had money, rationing prevented the purchase of any luxuries. My family were certainly hard up, but we were fortunate in that we had a wonderfully resourceful mother who could sew, knit, bake, cook and keep a large family very content and, as far as I was concerned, totally unaware of the hardship she endured. She was an extraordinary woman and it is to her I owe so much and only when I grew up and considered her week's work and her total dedication to her children did I understand her extraordinary achievements.

For my mother, wash day was a whole day's work, with the copper to be filled, the fire lit underneath and the sheets and clothes to be boiled. A huge old mangle wrung out the worst of the wetness between two massive wooden rollers before the washing was hung out to dry. Eventually this giant was replaced with a smaller wringer with slim white rollers. Monday was wash day and my mother had started long before we left for school and was still poking the full copper with the copper stick when we came back from school, glasses steamed up and her hands on her hips tired with an aching back. Tuesday was for ironing, and again with a large family it was a day long chore. The irons had to be heated till red hot and taken from the fire with tongs and slotted into the hefty iron casing. Clothes were raised and lowered on pulleys for airing in the living room. Since there was no electricity or running water it meant oil lamps lit the house. Ranges and wall ovens were for cooking and baking and water was pumped up or drawn from the well.

Everyone had to help get pails of water and with a big family it took a lot of pails to fill the copper on a Saturday for the weekly bath in a zinc tub. Little ones bathed in front of the fire whilst elder ones took their bath in the kitchen for a bit more privacy. Water for a bath could not be fresh for each person as it was just not feasible to fill, empty and refill at will. Washing on a daily basis was usually a frenetic affair with cold water in an outside wash house.

We had lovely fires in the living room, lit early by mother or one of the elder children and I even remember fires in the bedroom when we were ill. We loved hanging our feet out of bed and warming our toes. We never realized at the time what extra work it was for mother lugging coal up the stairs and having more grates to clean. My mother's day was long; she never stopped working. With only a wireless for the news, her evenings were spent sewing, knitting, mending or making something for the home. There was no time for indulgences or for herself. Only when I had children of my own and when I sometimes felt tired did I fully realize how hard my mother had worked for us all and her total unselfishness. She had no gadgets, no washing machine or electrical appliances when we were all small but she never complained. Sometimes if she had five minutes to spare she would come into the shed where we played and where there was a piano, and she would play and sing songs to us. Both she and my sister Joy could play the piano by ear and this is a lovely memory I have of Mum. Later when electricity and water were available and life became a bit easier I like to think Mum enjoyed her life with time for reading which she loved, and at last some time for herself. We spent hours as children in the harvest fields watching the binders cut the corn and the poor horse endlessly going round and round to work the elevator and thresh the corn. I can remember going to Wallage's farm fetching Lord Woolton's pies from the plump and rosy-cheeked Mrs Wallage who kept a stash of these in her cellar. We skipped for hours on Knapton Green and played with bat and balls in the fields. Seldom were we bored. 'No such thing as boring' Mum would say. 'No such word as can't.'

We had very little compared to children of today but we were content.

I remember my childhood as long summer days, walking for miles, biking if we had a bike to ride, or run behind, the kettle singing on the hob, my mother playing the piano, picking blackberries and primroses; true halcyon days. Days of blissful innocence.

The war did not impinge on my young life too much either. Perhaps it was because I was so young and was protected from the awful reality of war. I do remember the late night raids and the black-out blinds and our fear when we heard the doodlebugs chuntering ominously over the channel. So too I remember having to take our gas masks to school and having to practice wearing them. I also remember my big brother, Jimmy, in his army uniform and our excitement when he came home on leave and his letters from far flung places overseas. I have no doubt for my mother and older siblings, the war was far more grim and worrying; we younger ones as always were protected from this hideous knowledge.

My memories of Knapton School remain vivid and much cherished. Mrs Johnson was an exceptional teacher and like so many others I shall always be grateful to her for her endless patience and for being my teacher. I shall never forget the excitement of the trips to London and Blakeney and the hundred and one other things she packed into our education that remain with me today. It was Mrs Johnson who introduced me to asparagus and said one could dip the shoots into butter and eat them with fingers. I can hear her saying 'Even the Queen eats asparagus with her fingers'. I was most impressed and totally convinced that Mrs Johnson knew everything.

KATHLEEN JOHNSON (SUCKLING)
at Knapton School 1941 to 1948.

I really have no memories of being in the Infant Room with Miss Doughty. However the move into the Big Room is much clearer.

The room was separated into 2 classes with 7-11 sitting at the left hand side and the big children 11-14 sitting on the right hand side, with the teacher's desk more or less in the centre. (I think originally the room was divided by a curtain with a third teacher for the junior class. There were more children in those days and I have a feeling Trunch children came to Knapton. I have no idea when this changed.) The big children probably included the Ashley twins, Walter Pearman, Joy Lee, David Lee, Herbert Baines, Hazel and Reggie Smith, Jessie Rose and Tommy Rose. There were large desks with a bench seat attached on an iron arm, at the back of the room, where the eldest children sat. The rest of the desks were the normal pairs with chairs. I can remember when the leaving age rose to 14 and David Lee went off to the secondary modern school in North Walsham for his last year. There were 3 other children in my age group, Betty Wright, Brian Eastoe (GoGo) and Avril Edwards came to the school later.

The time table was hanging on the wall in a picture frame. In general one half of the class was being taught while the other half continued with various workbooks. So it was quite interesting to listen to the lesson while carrying on with the set work. The lesson would often be interrupted by someone needing help with a written task, but Mrs Johnson never seemed to be troubled by these breaks and everyone just got on with their work. I do remember being highly amused by a probably hungry boy, when asked what he needed replied, 'A piece of bread and butter, please', meaning a piece of blotting paper! (This was Edward Langham.)

We used to enjoy the 'wireless' lessons and always hoped the accumulator would hold out. (I have been trying to remember where we had to take them to be recharged, possibly the garage.)

My favourite program was 'Dylsford'. This was a country life/natural history program. Strangely enough 'Singing Together' with William Appleby has been mentioned on the radio this week in connection with the reintroduction of school singing lessons. We listened to 'How things began', and the Radio Doctor. 'Coughs and sneezes bring diseases,' springs to mind and something about 'a flying trapeze'.

I also remember being told to 'find a space' in 'Music and Movement'. These lessons gave us a taste of the outside world and presumably gave Mrs Johnson a break from continual teaching.

One of the joys of being ill when at the High School was being able to listen to these programmes again!

I think I enjoyed all my lessons at Knapton although I do remember complaining to Roger Dixon about 'these senseless sums'; the page of problems after each new stage. For children without baths and running water working out how long a bath, without a plug, would take to fill must have seemed a pretty futile

exercise. A favourite lesson was paper folding craft. We made boxes with lids, envelopes etc. I still have a purse/wallet, with a gusset, made out of strong brown paper. This was a way of teaching accurate measuring and was a preliminary of technical drawing.

The girls did needlework and I made two dresses. The first one was a Magyar style; only a back and a front and the short sleeves were cut in the main pieces. In my last year at Knapton I made a much more elaborate dress with a gathered skirt and set in sleeves. I can remember a lot of hand sewing but both dresses were well worn. We also had knitting lessons and I made a white polo sweater for a young cousin. We enjoyed making pom-poms using the cardboard milk bottle tops, winding the wool through the ready made hole.

Each day finished with another chapter from the book we were having read to us, we all looked forward to this and always hoped for a double instalment.

One thing I hated was school milk. In winter the crate of 1/3 pint milk bottles was put in front of the fire to warm up, which made it even less palatable for me though everyone else seemed to like it. On a good day I was able to give my milk to someone else without being seen by my mother.

The classroom must have been icy in the winter with only one large open fire. I don't remember being cold but do remember some children suffering from very painful chilblains on their hands and feet.

Also in the Big Room was a large glass-fronted bookcase which was the Village branch of the County Library. This was open to the villagers on Wednesdays after school. I think we children were allowed more access. It was always an excitement when the 'huge' Library van came and the books were replaced by newer titles.

Other visitors to the school were the nurse and the dentist. I remember lining up so the nurse could inspect our hair for nits and our hands for scabies. If she found any sufferers it was handled very discreetly as my first brush with nits was over 20 years later when my children were infected.

The dentist, Mr Packham, inspected our teeth at the side of the classroom. He returned with a caravan fitted out with terrifying equipment including a treadle operated drill. I can clearly remember having 2 milk teeth extracted and this experience put me off dentists for many years! He continued to look after my teeth until I left school at 18. After 11 I attended his surgery at the rear of the Secondary Modern School.

School Outings

One of the first outings I remember was a nature walk around Knapton. We walked down to Mr Wallage's pond, where we all joined in pond dipping. We collected frog-spawn, water snails to keep the tank clean, pond weed to aerate the water and daphnia for the tadpoles to eat. Later on when the tadpoles were well developed we brought small pieces of meat and hung them in the tank for the tadpoles to feed on. The tank had some large stones so that the frog-poles could get out of the water. Eventually we took the tiny frogs back to the pond.

At other times of the year on similar walks we collected wild flowers and later on, tree seeds and fruits. These were displayed on a nature table. We probably also collected birds eggs and nests.

Another very popular outing was to Blakeney Point to see the nesting terns and gulls. Mrs Johnson tried to arrange the date so that we walked across the marshes on the way out at low tide and then at the end of the day when we were all tired, the tide had come in and we were able to come back by motor boat. We were met on the point by the warden, Ted Eales, who made it all so interesting. After the first school outing here Mrs Johnson was asked by the parents if she could arrange an outing for parents as none of them had ever been there. I remember people coming back with bags of cockles and all being very enthusiastic about the day out. The soft mud squidging through toes was a new experience for most of them.

Each October we went to Yarmouth to see the herring fleet and watch the fisherwomen preparing herrings for salting. These would eventually turn into Red Herrings which were exported to Russia. Other herrings were gutted prior to smoking for kippers and bloaters.

One year the skipper of one of the boats invited us aboard to look around. I can still remember the smell of engine oil mixed with fish. We were amazed how much was packed into such a small space. The boat and crew had come from Buckie, in northern Scotland. After that we corresponded with the boat and crew and the link continued for many years. The captain certainly came to Knapton one year to look around the school and village.

For the senior children the highlight of the year was the outing to London. We left Knapton at 6.00 a.m. with a packed lunch and a little spending money, in a Starling's coach. Mr Johnson and Mrs Featherstone came as well. We had a comfort stop at Newmarket around 9.00 a.m. I remember buying a bag of cherries one year, and seeing the strings of racehorses another. Once in London we travelled around on the underground, quite a scary event for country children. Mrs Johnson rarely had problems with losing anyone as we were all rather clinging. One year we did lose a child. Mrs Johnson must have been in a panic but the girl, Margaret Self, was entertaining the local bobbies who returned her safely to the party. We went to Trafalgar Square, Buckingham Palace etc. always ending up at London Zoo. We were allowed to go off by ourselves having been shown the meeting point, and being told that on no account were we to go out of the turnstile. The coach picked us up outside the Zoo and we arrived home very tired about 11.00 p.m. I remember singing songs on the way home and thinking it was all very grown up.

The infants and juniors usually went to Cromer for a picnic on the beach. Even though Knapton was only 1 mile from the coast many children never went on the beach, so even this outing was often a new experience.

(Another early memory is of going to visit 'Aunty Gee', who lived in the council houses, about three doors from Ann Lee. She had been a teacher. Was she the third teacher at Knapton or the infant teacher before Miss Doughty? She had a sister Muriel who was badly disabled with cerebral palsy and I remember her being pushed around the village in a bath chair.)

The War

The actual war made very little impact on me. The shortage of sweets and exotic fruits was not a problem as I had never been used to them. As all the families grew their own vegetables and kept chickens, rabbits and some people had pigs our diet was not too bad. It would have been worse for the adults who were missing their tea, coffee and sugar. We did get Red Cross parcels from time to time which caused much excitement and pleasure. I think they came from Canada but can not remember exactly what they contained. I have a feeling it was things like dried fruit, soap, toothbrushes and sweets or small toys. They came in small, square, brown cardboard boxes and we were all very excited when they were distributed and eager to see the contents.

One group of evacuees arrived in Knapton from Bethnal Green very early in the war, 1940? We took in twin girls. (Their brother, who had left Liverpool Street on a different train ended up in North Walsham!) Their teacher came with them and their lessons were held in the Parish Room. After quite a short time, with the threat of a German invasion, Norfolk was considered too dangerous a place for these London children and so they were moved on. My mother thought if Norfolk was too dangerous for Londoners it was too dangerous for me, so I was sent to Yorkshire with my grandmother to stay with relatives. We were there for almost a year and I came home with a very broad Yorkshire accent. (The timing here is a bit vague as I know Daphne Lee was employed as child minder before I started school in Sep. 1941 or Jan. 1942, after my grandmother went to live in Kings Lynn.)

Later on the school was used by troops on manoeuvres. I can remember two occasions when the school was full of soldiers. Weekends or holidays? One of them kindly mended the brake on my doll's pram.

In 1944 with the flying bomb raids in London we had more evacuees in the village. I can remember one or two older girls joining our classes. (I can remember one girl quite clearly as she had a serious problem with BO and always smelled of boiled milk, poor thing.) Also a group of mothers with babies and small children arrived in Knapton. They had come from Leytonstone and were absolutely horrified and frightened in the village. No shops, no pubs or cinema, no street lights and wide open spaces. Within a very short time they decided it was better to die in London than die of boredom in Knapton. One family did stay and a lifelong friendship developed. Every summer a large black London taxi was seen outside the house of Nellie and Jack Kirk as the London family enjoyed a country holiday. (A few years ago Jill Watts' mother sent me a photo of Nellie and the London lady, still friends and both 80!)

About the same time my mother invited one of her friend's children to come and stay. However they had already been sent to Derbyshire. A few days later another friend asked if her little girl could come as she was very unhappy in her billet in Devon/Dorset. A few days after Phillipa arrived we had a call to say Edward and Josephine were very unhappy and could mum still have them and so they came too. It was really the best year of my life to have a younger sister (5) a twin sister (8) and an older brother (11). My mother had a seat on her bicycle for Pippa and the rest of us had our own cycles. I remember cycling to the beach and to North Walsham. (Quite often Gillian Watts was on these outings, but how did she travel?) The day the war ended I remember Josephine and me running down Hall Lane with Union Jacks, shouting to anyone we saw that the war had ended. The end of the war was celebrated with a dance in Mr May's barn which was swept out for the occasion. Then sadly my new family returned to London.

The other war memory concerned Miss Doughty. One Friday she told Mrs Johnson she was getting married the next day. After the usual pleasantries, Mrs Johnson asked what she would be called on Monday. After a few seconds of bewilderment, Miss Doughty replied that his name was Geoff, but she had no idea what his surname was.

During or soon after the war we did have the occasional windfall in jettisoned cargo from boats stuck on the Happisburgh sands. One boat had a cargo of tins of Players cigarettes which were much enjoyed by the local men. Another time a ship carrying whisky was beached. I remember my father and a group of men going out in the middle of the night and climbing down the cliffs near Bacton. Whether the tide was wrong or the Customs and Excise men too active they came back empty handed. (Was this a Home Guard exercise, I've often wondered!) In the early fifties we had great success with a cargo of oranges which were on their way to Newcastle for their Christmas quota. The customs men were not too interested in this cargo. Fruit could only be taken from damaged crates, but it was very easy to wade in and damage the crate before it was beached. We all had a very good feast as the fruit had not been in the water long enough to be spoiled. Because my mother and father were working all day we usually missed the very limited supply of fruit that was available in North Walsham so these oranges were a real treat.

During the war we were all encouraged to save. We had long thin cream coloured stamp books and bought either sixpenny stamps or expensive ones (two shilling or two and sixpenny ones, I'm not sure which). The two denominations were stuck on separate pages. When the book was full, it could be cashed in or transferred to savings Certificates or Post Office accounts. I used to go with my mother after school on Fridays to collect from some of the houses down Hall Lane. We ended up with Mrs Claydon who had always spent the afternoon baking and I can still remember the wonderful smell of warm baking in her big farm kitchen. Because every child in the school saved regularly we were awarded a certificate by the War Savings Committee (?) which was presented at the school by Lord Mackintosh of Halifax.

At some point my mother cooked dinners for the children. I can remember Valor oil stoves in the boys cloakroom and I think dishes such as stews and vegetable with steamed puddings to follow, were prepared. The big girls helped with the preparation and Miss Townsend came in to help serve the meal and wash up afterwards. This carried on until school meals were delivered from a central kitchen at Bacton. This service started before I left in 1948. Did we eat the meals at our desks? I can't remember any separate dining tables.

Soon after the war Miss Collier replaced Mrs Woodage/Doughty. In 1949 or 1950 she had a serious bicycle accident on her way to school. I used to meet her every morning on my way to the high school. On sunny morning she rode out of Crow Lane and straight into the path of one of Mr Tresize's taxis. I can still visualise her lying in the road, not a pleasant memory. She never recovered sufficiently to return to teach at Knapton. Luckily for the school Mrs Featherstone was persuaded to take the post, a year or two earlier than she had intended to return to teaching. She was known to Mrs Johnson as Mr Featherstone had completed his teaching practice at Knapton School in 1946 after an emergency Teachers Training Diploma following his naval war service. I think Wymondham College was used for this emergency training.

Knapton School house was built in 1902. It was very modest (small) with three bed rooms in a large garden. It was probably intended for a single lady with a maid! In some ways it was very advanced with an indoor water supply. The roof water from the school and the house was collected in a large underground tank. This fed a pump at the kitchen sink. One of the bedrooms had a wash hand basin with a drain. So although water had to be carried up, we could just pull the plug on the waste water. Drinking water was drawn up by a pump outside. This was a very deep bore tapping an underground stream about 70 feet down. Neither supply dried up during my time in the house. In cold weather it was sometimes necessary to thaw the outside pump with hot water before we could get a fresh supply.

There was a coal copper in the kitchen for wash days and a fireplace in all the other rooms. In the very rare cases of illness it was a special treat to have a fire in the grate in the bedroom. In the living room the heating took the form of a Triplex stove which had an oven above the open fire. I don't think this oven was often used for cooking as we had a Calor Gas cooker in the kitchen. We also used a Valor oil stove. My mother used to cook wonderful roast potatoes in a covered dish on top of the stove and at other times delicious steamed puddings. One of the snags of these stoves was that for no apparent reason the wick would flare and the stove would smoke. Returning to the kitchen, or in our case the back lobby, one would find the whole area covered in greasy black sooty cobwebs. The necessary cleaning up operation was not very pleasant, especially without the good cleaning agents we have to day.

Lighting was supplied by paraffin lamps with a tall glass chimney. The wicks had to be carefully trimmed and even so they still were known to smoke. Later on we had a Tilley lamp which gave out a much better light. These lamps had to be primed by methylated spirits and then pumped up to force the paraffin vapour up to the mantle to be burnt. These lamps gave a gentle hiss all the time they were in use. We had a Tilley radiant heater and a Primus stove which both worked on the same principle. It was possible to buy a Tilley storm lantern which could be taken outside.

I was born in Knapton School House in December 1936, just 2 days before my father's 41 birthday and 3 days before the abdication of Edward the eighth. My mother was attended by Dr Morrison and a live-in maternity nurse, who stayed for about a month. I am not sure how long her maternity leave lasted but I was told that my feeding routine was arranged to fit in with playtimes and dinner time! My mother was certainly a leader for women of the time. She was one of the first teachers allowed to continue after marriage, (she was married in December 1934), so being a working mother must have been even more unusual. For the first few years I was looked after by my grandmother, who lived with us. For a short while before I started school Daphne Lee became my childminder as my grandmother moved to King's Lynn to look after her other daughter who was ill.

Growing up in Knapton was an almost perfect childhood. During and just after the war there was virtually no motor traffic through the village, so we were safe to play in the roads. There were no strangers to worry about and everyone knew and cared for each other. This reminds me of an incident in the late forties. Mr Watts kept several hundred chickens on a field at the Mundesley end of Knapton and one night a number of these hens were stolen. At this time we had a fish and chip van which came round the villages weekly. Mr Ward had noticed a strange van in the area and he carefully recorded the number on the inside of his van. After hearing about the robbery he thought it worth mentioning his sighting to the police. When the registration number was checked and traced to a house visited in Leytonstone, it was found to be full of chickens! As Mr Watts' chickens had been treated with a wash they were identifiable and so were returned to him! We had no fears of walking about in the dark. There were no street lights in the village and everyone just went about their necessary business. The older people sometimes used torches but most didn't bother. I am sure my very good night vision is due to using my eyes at night as a child.

In some villages the landowners were oppressors but in Knapton, Miss Robinson, was very much The Lady of the Big House. In the days before social security and the N.H.S. it was said that most of the villagers wore false teeth and spectacles paid for by Miss Robinson. Every house was given a sack of coal at Christmas and all 'Church' girls received a very nice present on their wedding.

There were regular 'visitors' to the village. Every day except Sunday Mr Brighton cycled from North Walsham with the post. I have a feeling we even had a second post. If we had run out of stamps he was always willing to take the money, buy the stamp and post the letter for us. Quite often he would tell us who the letter was from.

Another visitor from North Walsham was Dr Morrison. I do not remember him coming very often although my father was prone to attacks of bronchitis and pneumonia having been badly gassed in the first world war. I do remember going to the surgery in North Walsham. The waiting room was quite small and dark. There were big medicine bottles on a shelf and it is the smell of the mixture of antiseptics and cough medicine that has left a lingering memory. Last time we passed through North Walsham I noticed that Morrison Close had been built in the garden and that the small waiting room door was still there, apparently unchanged.

We had regular deliveries of bread. The baker always had a large basket with a variety of loaves for us to select from. We were able to order groceries and later in the week they too would be delivered. I used to enjoy going to Cubitt's in North Walsham. Sugar was sold in blue paper bags. For small amounts the assistant would make a cone out of the same paper. (Even in the fifties when I was at the High School I used to buy a ¼lb of sultanas for 6d and these were weighed into a blue paper cone. By eating them one at a time I could make them last my whole cycle ride home!) Along the front of the counter were tins of the various biscuits with a glass lid which made for mouth-watering investigations. The other memories of this shop were the plain wooden boarded floor, and of course the smell of cheese, bacon and spices all mixed together.

Meat was also delivered twice weekly. We usually had a joint of beef, roast on Sunday, cold on Monday and cottage pie on Tuesday. We then had a stew which lasted for two days and I suppose vegetable dishes or fish filled in the other two days. Sometimes we had a chicken or a rabbit. Less frequently, if my father had been out shooting we would have wood pigeon. Not the variety one expects today.

Milk was delivered every day by Mr Puncher. We used to put a jug with a saucer on top out each evening. The next morning Mr Puncher would come round with a horse and cart carrying the churns of milk. He had a pint and a half pint measure, which were cylindrical in shape with a long handle which could be hooked over the lip of the churn. This delivery was discontinued before 1947. Milk could no longer be sold loose and buying bottling equipment would have been very expensive. The churns of milk were collected daily and the milk returned in pint bottles with a wide neck and a cardboard lid, with a pop out centre, to be delivered the next day. In the great snow of 1947 the milk lorries were unable to reach Knapton. This meant that Mr Puncher was unable to have his milk collected and his milk had to be emptied into the snow and of course no bottles of milk could be delivered for the villagers. When it was obvious the snow was going to be around for some time my mother made many phone calls and at last Mr Puncher was able to sell his milk direct to the villagers for the duration of the emergency.

The snow of 1947 was indeed an emergency. We had had snow several times in the January but on Feb. 9 we had a heavy fall coupled with very strong winds. That day my parents were returning home from King's Lynn. They got as far as the garage on the Cromer Road in Mundesley (Walpoles) and decided to abandon the car there and walk the rest of the way home, about 2½ miles. The next day the snow plough was able to get through and clear the road. My father walked back and collected the car. That night we had more snow and wind and no more traffic came through Knapton for 6 weeks. It was the wind that had caused the problem, blowing the fields clear and dumping the snow in the roads, level with the top of the hedges to a depth of about six feet. The drift in Hall Lane started just past the School House. There was also a huge drift on the school lawn which John Wild and I dug out to make a den. The boys' playground had also blown clear and was a sheet of black ice. This made a wonderful skating rink for us to play on. Cars were almost buried in snow on the roads and either in 1941 or 1947 a train was stuck near Knapton station. This train was carrying oxygen cylinders for the sanatorium at Mundesley. Sledges were brought out of sheds and stores to take them on to Mundesley. (Dr Gutch at Knapton Hall loaned a very good, large one.) The sledges were also used by the men of the village who walked to Mundesley over the fields to bring back bread and other goods in sacks to keep us fed. The school was closed for some of the time. It would have been too difficult for small children to walk through the snow. After some time German prisoners of war were drafted in to dig walk ways through the drifts. I can remember they used stones to write 'We want to go home' in the snow walls.

Luckily in those days we were prepared and every house would have had a shed full of coal and a good log pile so we were able to keep warm. Paraffin for the lamps and oil stoves was probably more of a problem, and probably had to be carried back from Mundesley

The School House had its own problem. The wrong sort of snow was around even then! In this case it was very fine dry snow. When this snow fell in conjunction with a strong wind the snow was forced under the tiles into the roof space. This happened in 1941 and when the thaw came, the weight of wet snow brought one of the bedroom ceilings down. After that the Education Committee cut a hatch into the roof space. In 1947 my father, helped by neighbours, removed 120 buckets of snow from the loft! Even so when the thaw came I can remember going to bed covered with a tarpaulin and hearing the drip, drip of snow melt into various bowls and buckets placed at appropriate places around the bed rooms.

Winter was a lonely time for an only child. The evenings were seemingly long. We did of course have a wireless set. In the forties and fifties Children's Hour was broadcast every evening from 5.00 p.m. to 6.00 p.m. Some days were more interesting than others. Norman and Henry Bones, the boy detectives, was my favourite programme. 'Toytown' with Larry the Lamb never really appealed to me although I usually listened. There were nature and science programmes, quizzes and serialized books. In fact something for most tastes. In the evening my favourite programme was 'Dick Barton, Special Agent'. This was broadcast every evening at quarter to seven for quarter of an hour. The Friday episode always finished on a cliff-hanger leaving me on tenterhooks over the weekend. I can remember being devastated when the programme was axed. We also listened to 'Much Binding in the Marsh' and 'Round the Horn'. On Saturday we listened to 'In Town Tonight'. The programme was introduced by the music of Eric Coates' march Knightsbridge. After 'stopping the sound of London traffic' interesting people who were 'In Town Tonight' were interviewed. On Sundays the wireless was carried into the front room where we listened to the Music from the Palm Court Orchestra. I still think of the Paul Temple detective serials whenever I hear Coronation Scott. As a teenager I was an avid listener of Radio Luxembourg. This was a commercial programme with adverts. We listened to quiz programmes and of course pop music on this wave length. Later on The Goons was the weekly favourite, probably the last really good programme before television took over.

We played cards frequently. Rummy and Newmarket were my favourites. Instead of money we used home-grown haricot beans for the stakes! When I was older I spent many hours playing cribbage with my father. Reading, colouring and playing with my dolls filled in the rest of the evenings. When I was about eleven I started knitting, mainly clothes for my dolls. Later on I took dolls' outfits into Mundesley and sold them in Mrs Lebell's shop. The proceeds paid for more wool.

Winter did have some compensations. I used to love looking out of my bedroom window on sharp frosty nights to look at the stars. There was no light pollution in those days. Occasionally we would be rewarded with a glimpse of the northern lights. We did not get the colours seen further north but more of a shimmery glow in the northern sky. In the morning we would wake up to find frost patterns covering the window glass. It was fun to blow on the ice and then watch the fingers of ice growing across again. This was much more fascinating than getting into an iced-over car which is the best children can do these days.

Also in the winter we had Valentine's Day. After school we would rush home to see if Father Valentine had been, and of course he hadn't. We would wait with increasing anticipation for the knock on the front door. At last the knock came and on running to the door and opening it we would find a small gift on the step such as a painting book or some crayons. We never found out who came and nobody ever saw Father Valentine! This must have been a custom very local to Knapton as I have never met anyone else who had such a visitor.

My abiding spring memory is of picking primroses on the railway bank near Knapton station. We tried to pick as many buds as possible. The flowers were carefully bunched and then wrapped in damp tissue paper and moss before being packed in a small cardboard box and sent by post to an aunt in Bradford.

When petrol became more available, a drive to the cherry orchards at Westwick was an annual favourite. We also used to go to Witton Woods to see and, in those days, pick bluebells. As a teenager I remember biking to the woods but as a smaller child we must have used the car.

Summer was a wonderful time. My mother and I spent many hours on the beach at Mundesley. Even though there were barricades along the promenade to prevent vehicles landing, local people were allowed access to the beach all through the war. We had to use the main entrance by the Coastguard building. During the years of double summertime we were often on the beach early enough for the sun still to be shining low on the sea, making for a wonderful sparkle. I eventually learned to swim the year the war ended and have enjoyed swimming ever since. In those days the beach was usually quite empty, as of course there were no holiday makers and not many local people seemed to enjoy the sands.

At harvest time we used to join the men in the fields to watch the binder at work. First of all men had to cut round the edge of the field with scythes to make room for the horse-drawn binder. As the sheaves of corn were thrown out the bigger children used to help make the stooks. These were double rows of about 12 sheaves arranged to let the corn dry out before being built into a stack. As the standing corn got smaller and smaller with the binder working towards the centre of the field, the men with dogs and sticks would be ready to catch the rats and rabbits when they had to break out of cover. After a few days the corn was ready to stack. The sheaves were loaded onto horse-drawn wagons and taken to the stack yard or the edge of the field to be built in a stack and usually given a thatched roof to keep the rain out. In later years just a tarpaulin was thrown over. One of the best jobs on the farm was to be a 'Hold Ye' boy leading the horses. I was never able to do this as tractors had taken over before I was old enough. We often took picnics to eat in the field. The men would always welcome a can of tea. Not the can we think of today but an enamelled can holding about a pint and a half with a lid and a loop handle. The dust from the corn made for very thirsty work. Harvest must have been very hard work for the men as they worked very long days, almost dawn to dusk when the weather was dry, but it was great fun for the children. We would return home with our legs badly scratched by sharp corn stalks and very tired and hungry.

Another summer memory would horrify mothers today! Clothes and shoes were hard to come by, and expensive, in the post-war years. We usually had one pair of shoes for winter and a pair of sandals for summer. For playing in, we cut the toes out of the top of the sandal of the last year's pair which gave room for our bigger feet for another summer! In the summer we played outside most of the day. Ball games were very popular and the large blank wall on the side of the school was ideal. We had a sequence game involving throwing the ball against the wall and catching it again. We had to throw under a leg, round our back, catch with one hand and so on. This was onesy. Having completed this sequence we moved on to twosy, using two balls but my memory fails in what we were expected to do! We used to spend a lot of time doing handstands. I was very envious of Josephine Langham who could go over into a crab and complete excellent cartwheels. I was really too stiff and gangly to be much good at this but enjoyed it nevertheless. Josephine also introduced us to playing jacks or dabs. This involved throwing up a small stone and then picking up other stones before catching the original one. Again a sequence was involved.

After the war when cars became more frequent I remember sitting for hours on the wall at the cross roads collecting car numbers! We were all expert on the various makes and models of cars passing by. In a similar vein we also used to collect film-star photographs. It was very good practice for our letter-writing skills as we must have written many letters asking for signed photos.

Harvest Festival was one of my favourite Church services. The church was filled with fruit and vegetables and great sheaves of corn. The ladies always made a wonderful display and then we from Sunday school took along our small offerings.

With autumn came the fruits on the hedgerows. We used to go around the fields and down the lanes picking blackberries. A walking stick was a must for hooking down the high brambles. The best fruit were always just out of reach. Once home the fruit would be cooked and the juice drained through a cloth to be made into delicious bramble jelly, to join the other preserves on the shelf for winter.

We used to make another expedition to Witton Woods to pick up sweet chestnuts which we would then roast in front of the fire. We would also collect horse chestnuts for playing conkers. I don't remember anyone getting injured. It seems such a shame that children today are stopped from such pursuits. We also used horse chestnuts for making doll's house furniture. Pins were used for chair legs and chair backs again used pins with thread woven around to fill in the spaces. This furniture only lasted a few months as the conkers dried out and became dull and misshapen. (More durable was furniture made out of match boxes. These were excellent for chests of drawers.

During autumn the giant threshing machines would be hauled into the village by a traction engine. The stacks of corn would be fed into machine so that the grain was separated from the straw. The corn used to pour out of a spout into hessian sacks and the straw would be made into stacks again to be stored until it was needed for bedding for the livestock. As the corn stack was dismantled nests of field mice used to be uncovered.

One of Mr Wallage's grand-daughters and I spent many happy hours collecting up the tiny pink baby mice, the size of jelly babies and putting them into nurseries.

As autumn merged into winter we were busy thinking about Christmas. Although presents were an important part we were not so materialistic as the children nowadays and were very pleased with small presents. Books always featured on my wish list and during the war and for a few years after were very difficult to come by, and often had to be ordered from Jarrolds in Norwich months ahead.

In those days everyone made their own mincemeat, puddings and cakes. Bought ones were far too expensive for most village folk and home-made was definitely the order of the day. Most people had a home-grown chicken or a local turkey for the Christmas meal. My father would have plucked the bird; this was definitely an outside job as the fine under feathers flew everywhere. I can remember my father and uncle drawing sinews from the turkey legs to make carving easier. My mother would draw the innards from the bird. This then had to be singed by holding it over a dish of flaming methylated spirits to remove the fluff left after plucking. Oven-ready still had to be invented! My job was to make the bread crumbs for the stuffing by rubbing day-old bread round and round a colander. This was extremely hard on young hands.

In other ways the rest of the meal was much as it is today. I do remember experimenting with various recipes for mock cream to go with the pudding. One of the less successful involved beating a small amount of butter (margarine) and sugar into a bowl of made-up cornflour mould. My favourite was whipped-up evaporated milk, closely followed by thickly mixed milk powder.

After eating this enormous meal at midday we would sit down again in the evening to a huge cold supper of pork pie and haslet, salads and bread followed by a large sherry trifle. As we always went to King's Lynn to stay with my aunt and uncle, we were not able to join the Christmas service at Knapton Church.

And so the years passed by, closely following the agricultural calendar. We always seemed to have things to do, and village people were always supportive of each other. We had a sense of community which these days seems to be sadly lacking.

WILLIE PUNCHER
at Knapton School 1942 to 1951

I can remember the Church Sunday School in the Parish Room. A Sunday School was held in the Chapel.

Electricity came to the village in 1946, and before that, my mother cooked in a coal-fired wall oven and an oil stove. She did our shopping mostly at the Co-op in North Walsham, which delivered once a week. I thought our Christmas dinner was a real treat. I can remember the coupon books in the war, so many coupons for a pound of butter or sugar, meat bread and cakes etc.

At home, we had a vegetable garden, and kept rabbits. One of my jobs was collecting food for them.

I can remember church fêtes always held at Miss Robinson's. The activities included darts, bean bags, hoop-la, kicking a football to burst balloons tied to a large door, bowling for the pig. There must have been a few more that I can't remember.

The Men's Club was built by the men of the village. The main two were Henry Wild, carpenter, and Bob Wright, bricklayer. A number of other men also helped out. It was completed in 1950. Above the door is a cement block with 1950 on it. Behind this block is a piece of paper in a sealed tin with all the names of the men who helped build the Club.

Mains water came to the village in 1956. Mains sewerage never came; the only houses to have mains sewerage are the two lots of council houses. Water was drawn from either a well or a pump from deep in the ground. Some were 80 foot or more deep. There must have been 10 or 12 wells or pumps in the village. As far as toilets were concerned, everyone had to go to the privy at the bottom of the garden. When it was full, a hole was dug in the garden. Later on, the council came in the night with a motor tanker and emptied the toilet. This was known as the honey cart. Now everyone has their own septic tank and soak-away.

74

I can remember watching the Lancaster bombers in the war, dozens of them going over to Germany. Also standing in the yard at night and hearing the doodlebugs going over.

I think it was 19 January 1947 when it started to snow, and it went on for weeks freezing all the time. An easterly wind blew the snow into the roads. Hall Lane was one big block of snow to a depth of over six foot. Men who were on the dole were sent to clear the road by shovel, but no sooner had they cleared it than the wind blew more off the fields so they started all over again. I helped to clear part of Hall Lane near the railway bridge so my father could take the horse and cart to get some cattle food. He also took milk to the village by sledge. All the other roads in Knapton were as bad as Hall Lane.

I was at North Walsham school when the King died. We were in the middle of a lesson when the news came through. The grumpy old teacher said, 'All right, he's done his duty, now get on and do yours'.

We were badly affected by the 1953 floods. I can remember going to Bacton and walking on the beach to Walcot. We saw all the damage to the houses. It was said that if you had stood on the front at Mundesley, you would have got wet by the splash of the sea.

The first combine I saw working was at Mr Norman May's, Church Farm, Knapton, around 1948 to 1950. It was a Marshall and was pulled by a tractor, a lot different from the monsters of today. Steam threshing had taken place on all seven farms in Knapton. Threshing contractors who came to Knapton were Mr Gooch of Bacton and Mr Aldridge of Worstead. When Mr A was threshing, some men from the other farms went to help, and then it was vice versa. When I was at school I would hurry home and that would be the time the day's threshing was coming to an end, and we armed ourselves with large sticks as there were a lot of rats and mice to catch. When the steam threshing machine travelled through Hall Lane, my cousin and I liked to get on the railway bridge. The weight limit was 10 tons, but nothing ever happened.

In the summer evenings of the 50s, 60s, and 70s the boys and girls of the village would gather at the cross roads and have a chat and tell jokes. Some were a bit blue. One night a car came round the corner from North Walsham to Mundesley at speed. He must have just filled up with petrol and forgotten to put the petrol cap on, so petrol gushed out round the corner on to the road. Us boys got a box of matches, struck one, and dropped it on the petrol – Whoosh, the flames went about 10 foot high for about 30 yards. It was all over in about 10 to 15 seconds. Now on summer evenings none of the young ones meet on the corner. I expect they are all at home with their own telly, phone, play station etc.

The boys also liked to collect cigarette cards which were in Turf cigarettes. Some packets had football stars, cricketers, rugby players etc. We all tried to get a set by swapping for different cards. We also liked to collect car numbers. In those days if you saw 10 cars in Hall Lane per day you were lucky, now you can see 10 in 10 minutes. How times have changed.

The railway which served Paston and Knapton was opened in 1898. In its heyday, it was very busy. A lot of children from Mundesley, Paston and Knapton used the train to get to school at North Walsham, and people used it to get to work or go shopping. The freight traffic on the line was very busy from late September till late January with sugar beet. There were at least 14 farmers from Paston, Bacton, Edingthorpe, and Knapton who took their beet to the station and forked them into trucks. That was hard work. The train took the beet to Cantley near Acle. Incoming goods traffic was beet pulp, that is beet that had been shredded and the sugar taken out. It was used for cattle feed. Fertiliser, seed potatoes and coal also came in. The coal was for Mr J. Gooch of Bacton, and Mr J. Larke of Knapton who had a coal round in the village.

The station master was a Mr Elijah Coe. The last few years, it was Mr Harrison. Not long after the line closed the track was taken up and some of the ground was sold. One section of the cutting in Hall Lane was filled in and a house built upon it. The section from Hall Lane to North Walsham is now a footpath. I have the old signal box from the station standing in my garden.

Mr Small was a carpenter in the village and Mr Bussey was the blacksmith. They both lived and worked in the Street. Mr Tom Coe was the roadman for the village. Now all three trades have gone. Mr Ward of Mundesley came to the village one evening a week with a fish and chip van stopping on the corner.

Elijah Coe, stationmaster of Knapton and Paston Station, with his father

Before electricity came to the village, your radio was powered by a small battery delivered by Mr Bridges of Mundesley. A full charged one was left one week, then next week it was taken away to be recharged and another full one was left. Some meat was delivered in the village by Mr Palmer from North Walsham, Mr Frostick, Mundesley, and Mr Bird from Southrepps.

A lot of men would spend Sundays out with their dogs, ferrets, nets and guns catching rabbits for their families to eat in the week ahead. Bread was delivered by Mr Hewitt, Mundesley, and Fayers of North Walsham.

My father, Mr Puncher, had a small dairy herd and sold some of the milk around the village in the 30s, 40s, and 50s. The milk was in two small churns on a trade bike with two measures, one pint and a half pint to measure out what people required in their jugs. Mr Twigg of Mundesley also had a milk round. Now Dairy Crest bring milk in, but customers are few and far between, as a lot of people go to the supermarket.

Mr Pike of Trunch and Mr Taylor of Black Cat Garage, in North Walsham, delivered paraffin for cooking and oil lamps.

Eastern Counties buses served the village. The pick-up point was on the Green to go to Mundesley via Trunch and Gimingham, or North Walsham then to Norwich via Wroxham. Now a private company runs two or three buses every day.

Every farm in the village and surrounding villages had cattle. Now, because of falling returns and ever-increasing rules and regulations, no one in the same area has got cattle now.

Since 1945, 81 new houses have been built in Knapton, 9 old barns and out-buildings have been converted to dwellings. Knapton House, Miss Robinson's old home, has been converted to flats. Even the old school where we all learnt the ABC is now a dwelling.

SHIRLEY WRIGHT (CONQUEST)
at Knapton School 1943 to 1953

Knapton School - Buildings
I remember the Big Room where children from the age of 7 - 14 worked in this one room and Mrs Johnson had to teach all lessons to all different ages and quite often had to blow her whistle to get our attention. In the winter the large heavy radiators used to warm our milk which was quite often delivered frozen. The cloakrooms were full of coats, hats, etc. and

77

were very cold probably due to the bare concrete floors. The kitchen was kept very clean and I don't think we were allowed in there. The outside toilets were very basic and very cold in the winter but we did not have any other option.

The playground was quite large for a village school and at playtime we all managed to occupy ourselves with various activities such as noughts and crosses, hopscotch, skipping etc. and more team games as we got older. We all took a great interest in the school garden as we produced quite a few flowers and vegetables, I enjoyed that. I remember the piano, and we had to all join in with the singing.

The people
Mrs Johnson – I realise now how hard she must have worked having to teach all subjects to all 20 pupils at different ages. She was quite serious and quite strict but always encouraged us to take an interest in our school work and was very keen to introduce us to other various activities, such as competing with other schools on sports days, competitions for wild flower collecting, entering our paintings in a national savings competition (I think this was correct).

Mrs Doughty – I cannot remember but think perhaps she could have been my first infant school teacher.

Mrs Breeze – A lovely teacher who was a gentle and kind who also accompanied us on day trips to London.

Mr & Mrs Featherstone – Both very nice teachers - Mr Featherstone very tall and slim and Mrs Featherstone very small and slim.

Miss Townsend – Very serious and strict but always organised and calm, and Mrs Watling produced some very nice dinners, especially the chocolate sponge pudding and chocolate sauce and something called pig's fry, but I don't think I could eat pig's fry now!

The Dentist. I remember the caravan in the school playground and once having to have two teeth extracted. I was terrified, he seemed quite an oldish man to me at the time and his breath smelling heavily of tobacco.

Lessons
I enjoyed all kinds of sports and taking part in the county sports days. Needlework was also a favourite especially when Mrs Johnson taught me how to smock and I eventually produced a small cotton gingham frock with smocking, for my niece aged two. Another challenging lesson was a competition each week to work in pairs and to see who could collect the most and the rarest wild flowers and I think the incentive was to be given

gold stars to the winners. I think those gold stars were as important to some of us as being real gold. It made us work hard!

I remember those lovely summer days when we would take our desks out into the playground and work, putting up with the breeze that constantly blew our papers around, but it was certainly worth it. The weather always seemed to be warm and sunny.

The Scholarship

I remember taking the scholarship exams at Mundesley school which, at the time, I was so pleased to have passed as I had always enjoyed English, Maths, etc. at school, but my biggest disappointment was when, having been interviewed by the Headmistress at North Walsham High School I was not accepted. I was quite upset at the time as it was my aim to go to the High School, so had to stay at Knapton school until the age of 14 and then to North Walsham Secondary School for the one year. I really did enjoy that school, taking part in whatever was going on, such as the drama group and acting in the school play, geography weeks in Derbyshire, music lessons, English lessons and especially maths which would have taken me into the advanced maths class had I completed the whole year, but I had taken an exam to go to Norwich City College, which I passed and therefore was only at the North Walsham school for two terms, but it was a great experience because the number of pupils in the classes made you work harder if you wanted to achieve good results.

The School Year

Making Christmas decorations was quite a festive time of the year with the coloured paper chains, and cutting into half a potato to make a pattern to use as a stencil and I think we even had Christmas pudding. (I can't believe I'm remembering all this!) The school garden was lovely and the excitement of growing pinks and taking them round the village to sell to make money for the school funds was a little competitive and as I was not content to just sell to local people, I cycled to Mundesley with another girl (can't remember who) and thought I would sell more if I went to Mundesley Holiday Camp and knocked on the chalet doors and managed to sell all mine. Thinking that Mrs Johnson might be pleased with my results was not quite the outcome and I was told I must never do that again. I can't remember if I was awarded one of those gold stars, probably not.

School dinners and milk

I remember drinking milk from small bottles, a third of a pint, each day and had to thaw them out on the radiators in the winter. I stayed to school dinners which were mostly quite nice.

Getting to school

I did not live far from school so I walked with other children who lived near me and it took 10 minutes.

Outings

The outings to London were very interesting for us. You had to be 10 years old and upwards.

We went by coach and had to leave at 6 a.m. Each year we were taken to all the different tourist attractions and I think going to London was the highlight of our school year. I think I spent most of my pocket money on ice creams, I don't know why.

One year we went when the Festival of Britain was on, can't remember which year (1951). That was something different. Mrs Johnson worked so hard organising these trips and it gave us the opportunity to learn so much about London and what it was like to visit a very big city. I will always remember these outings and the variety of places we were taken. Blakeney Point was something different, we had to go by boat from Morston out to the point and walk back providing the tide was out, which Mrs Johnson would obviously obtain this information beforehand. It was so peaceful out there and amazing how the birds would lay their eggs on the sand where we would have to tread so carefully, and on walking back we would gather cockles in the slimy black slippery mud often falling over and getting quite dirty. On one trip I gathered quite a few cockles in a small sack but somehow on the way back, lost them. This was also a lovely day out. All the other outings such as sports days and singing and dancing festivals were very enjoyable.

Knapton Village

Knapton Church always held Sunday services one week in the morning and the next week in the evening. I was in the choir and Miss Robinson, who lived at Knapton House, was the organist. The Reverend Thur was the rector during the time I was there and he officiated at my wedding. We attended Sunday School in the Parish Hall each Sunday and then went on to Church. There was usually a Sunday School outing to Great Yarmouth in the summer where we would go by train. Also there was a Christmas party. Miss Townsend and Mrs Dixon were the Sunday School teachers. A few of us when we reached the age of around 15 would also go to the Methodist chapel for a Sunday service alternating with the Church Service. Mr and Mrs Herbert Hicks who were Methodists and lived near the Parish Hall at Goodrest, would hold a Youth Group at their house once a week and also an invitation back to their house on a Sunday evening. We were all made so welcome and they really enjoyed having us as we were a good crowd and got on so well together, we would often have evenings out, such as visiting their farm for supper, a walk along the beach from Bacton to Mundesley in the summer evenings or going to other activities at other Methodist groups. We always spent part of the evening discussing religion. It was lovely to participate with other people of the same age and gave us something to occupy our time in such a quiet village. The shop was very well supported and I remember nearly everything was purchased in brown paper bags.

I remember going on a Saturday afternoon with other girls to Mrs Wilkinson's bungalow (the wife of Major Wilkinson) who lived in one of the bungalows (the last one at the time) along the Mundesley Road at Knapton where she taught us how to play croquet, hoping, I think, to introduce a little refinement into our lives. It was nice to be given the opportunity to learn how to play it and spend the afternoon with other girls enjoying refreshments etc. in her garden. She was quite an elegant lady and very nice.

Every year there was a Church fête which was held at Miss Robinson's house and lovely garden. We would always go and would always be given a job to do. Also there was always a Methodist Church fête at the home of Mr and Mrs May at Church Farm in the Street. This was always held on Whit Monday. Our youth group would always help and would go to the farm kitchen in the morning where we would prepare the food for the afternoon teas at the fête and we would also help in the afternoon. This was great fun, working together as a team.

At Christmas our youth group would put on a nativity play in the Parish rooms and we would also put on a concert in the summer at various Parish halls.

I remember there were socials at the Parish Hall and I remember there were sometimes barn dances, I think in one of Mr May's Barns. This was something a little different and attended by quite a few people.

Lastly I remember weddings at the church, I was one of those people who got married there and I expect there are a few more who also did the same.

When I was a child there was no electricity and we had to use oil lamps that constantly smoked if the wick was not trimmed. We did not have running water and had to fetch this from a well or pump in buckets which was situated and shared between the 12 council houses where I lived. Sanitation was very primitive and outside toilets with buckets had to be emptied each week in the garden, and on a moonlit night this would be the task of the male members of the household.

On a sweeter note, food rationing I remember, as I was allowed 4 ozs of sweets per week and I would have a treat and cycle down to Mundesley to Miss Earl's sweet shop in the High Street to choose my 4 ozs, and then cycle back home again, usually on a Saturday morning. We had a large garden at home and my father would grow lots of lovely vegetables as he was a keen gardener and I think my interest in gardening stems from him.

One of the meals I used to enjoy was getting fish and chips from a van belonging to a Mr Ward which came round to the villages at tea time during the week, I think Knapton on a Wednesday and Trunch on a Friday. Very popular.

My mother used to mainly shop in North Walsham, getting the bus from the Green at Knapton and buying at the International Stores.

JOSEPINE LANGHAM (HOURAHANE)
at Knapton School 1944 to 1945

In the Summer 1944 German V1s (Robot Bombs) and V2s (Rocket-powered ballistic missiles) were used to bombard British mainland.

My brother Edward and I, Josephine, were 2 of 1000s of children moved from the war-torn London suburb of Worcester Park. An unforgettably long train journey from Epsom to Stockport, with no changes, amazing!

Our parents knew Mrs Johnson (Miss Wilson) in the late 1920s and had spent holidays with her and Jenny her sister, in Fakenham and on The Broads. So when Aunty Kitty heard of the unsuitable billets in Cheshire she offered to have us join her family at School House in Knapton. It was to be the beginning of a love affair with Norfolk and especially Knapton and her family. No more sleeping rough in cupboards, home-erected Morrisons or school shelters. We loved the fresh air, open fields, local food and especially school, Knapton School, Aunty Kitty and Uncle Arthur and Kathleen were wonderful and made us part of their family, together with Pippa Ballard (aged 4) who sadly we have lost touch with. Looking back over that year we considered ourselves very lucky evacuees. Our parents must have been very relieved to know we were safe, and out of earshot of the dreaded air raid warning sirens.

Knapton School

A lovely village school, red brick country design in a perfect setting in which to learn and play safely, I really only knew the BIG ROOM, we did not roam far from our desks in school time. My desk was in front of Aunty Kitty who I had to call Mrs Johnson. The massive clock kept good time, the fire burned brightly but the high windows were well out of our reach.

It was a peaceful learning area. Mrs Johnson was an all-round expert, she played the piano for all our singing, organised and taught us country dancing and P.E. Her gardening skills she passed on to the boys especially; each had a plot to cultivate. I was very proud of the raffia/wool slippers I made in the craft lesson. I can still knit on 4 needles thanks to her, of course she taught a whole range of subjects to a full class of mixed ages 7-14 and mixed abilities. But we all made progress. Previous to this regular teaching I had spent most of my school day in the air-raid shelters. Much of my basic early learning improved by being in Knapton School. My brother progressed too and years after gained his Ph.D. in meteorology and later emigrated to Canada. By the 1970s he became a director in the Canadian Space Agency. I qualified as a teacher at Digby Stuart Roehampton in 1956, never teaching at Knapton as I innocently hoped, but held many good posts before retiring in 1986. Mrs Johnson encouraged us all and she would have been proud of every one of her pupils whatever course in life he or she took.

North Walsham's Catholic Church was too far for us to attend so Miss Mary Kiernan of Old Knapton Hall took us to Mundesley where Mass was said for the servicemen in the Grand Hotel/Continental.

St Peter and Paul Knapton Church well-known for its hammer beam roof was and is a well-loved church. Kathleen Johnson was married there in April 1960, I remember it well. The shop - oh the shop! It was not opened as a shop in 1944-45 but Mrs Dixon let us play shops with Pamela and Barbara; after the war it became a much welcomed village store again.

Knapton villagers made their own entertainment and we children joined in. Miss Robinson and Miss Leather opened their house and gardens, Knapton Hall, to host a garden fête. Everyone was so friendly and sociable. I became an elf for the fancy dress show! No doubt the costumes came from school. Mr May of Church Farm allowed a barn to be used for the Village Barn Dances. I am sure a few marriages were sparked off from these.

We walked or biked everywhere. The car had been immobilised during the war. We each had bikes of a sort except Pippa who travelled in a basket chair on the back of Aunty Kitty's bike.

We did go to Fakenham once or twice although I am not sure how. But I do remember having a typical Yorkshire lunch with the Yorkshire puddings first and then the meat and veg second, at Rose Cottage, home of Aunty Maud and Uncle Walter (Priest). The beach at Mundesley was out of bounds and I seem to remember certain safe places because Aunty Kitty taught me to swim, and many others too. Another of her skills!

A typical school day started with a good breakfast - cereal and bacon and egg cooked on the primus stove. The indoor pump supplied all but drinking water. That was drawn from a deep outside well. Five of us used the one outside bucket W.C. Fortunately the school toilets were not far away.

Every meal was laid properly at the table with ringed serviettes - none of today's casual habits. Most of our food was locally produced. The milk delivered daily from Mr Puncher was left in jugs on the doorstep. The butcher and baker called weekly with the order. We had no snacks in between meals - a praiseworthy habit. Every night we had a story read to us by the light of a mantle lamp. Enid Blyton's *Faraway Tree* was a favourite and often re-enacted on the stairs. The winter of 1944 was pretty and severe, snow was blown into hedge-high drifts - quite spectacular. We skated on the pond too with no fear. Mind you we were being supervised; Aunty Kitty took on a great responsibility, having 3 extra children to care for with no obvious end in sight but she did it patiently and with total commitment.

Soon after V.J. day 15 August 1945 we returned home to Surrey - quite a different scene from lovely Knapton. We were invited to return and stay at School House whenever we could, so every summer holiday until 1960 I spent in Knapton and loved it. We swam, cycled, played tennis, fruit-picked. Our holiday at the canning factory came to a hasty end as I sliced part of my finger in a bread slicing machine, never did find the slice! Both Aunty Kitty and Kathleen fainted at the sight of it!

My husband-to-be spent time in Knapton but since there was no room in School House he slept in the school, a first time experience for him - never to be forgotten. Throughout the days of evacuation and beyond, Aunty Kitty and Uncle Arthur were always calm, cheerful and so kind. I think of them often. They saved our lives in more ways than one.

More of Knapton from Jo Langham (Hourahane)

Before evacuation, our lives were dominated by air raids, sirens, doodlebugs, gas masks and the all clears but I cannot say that I was ever frightened. As I was only 3 when war broke out I knew no other way of life. Our parents never left us alone neither were we hungry. The worst rationing came at the end of the war. We kept a few chickens but only the number each family was allocated. If oranges or bananas came to our local grocers I would queue for hours to get our ration. Our ration books went with us to Knapton so at least School House gained a little from our presence. My mother had to work once we were evacuated and among her many different jobs one was in a bakery. So she would often send a parcel of various cakes and rolls to Knapton. No doubt there were other goody parcels sent so we were never hungry.

Rations per person per week were roughly, 1 oz cheese, 2 ozs butter, 2 ozs tea, 4 ozs bacon or ham, 8 ozs sugar, meat 1 shilling's worth. Bread, sugar and clothes were still rationed well after the war.

We had fresh milk delivered daily from Mr Puncher, fresh vegetables from the garden, and a weekly delivery of all other groceries from N. Walsham. Friday was baking day. Yes we lived much better than most. In fact we cannot remember seeing a doctor or dentist or even spending a day in bed ill.

Farming in Knapton demanded hard work, long hours, low wages from a number of devoted labourers reaping the harvest. Every job was labour-intensive before the introduction of all things mechanical. No doubt Knapton has moved on after 60 years but I cherish living in those happy days in the 40s.

Christmas 1944

In school we made our own cards and calendars. I well remember the stencils we used to decorate Christmas paper. The Johnson family went to King's Lynn that year so that our parents could spend Christmas with us. Another kind gesture.

Sadly many evacuees never saw their parents after the war. I have always felt blessed for being spared that grief.

Our house in Worcester Park only had minor bomb damage. A ceiling fell and dented a dressing table which I still have.

We stopped going to our parish church because the way there passed bombed houses. Those areas were out of bounds.

Going to church on Sunday was not always a priority at School House. Aunty Kitty would say 'Your God won't mind if you miss Mass'. Later on, a Sunday coach from Mundesley to N. Walsham would pick us

85

up at Knapton and drop us off at the Catholic Church. Josie and Brian Watts were among the travellers.

Valentine's Day was observed at School House. Maybe in other households too. There would be a knock at the front door. No one would be there but a small gift left for each of us. We discovered years later that Uncle Arthur rigged up a scheme whereby he could rattle the letter box without leaving the back kitchen. We all thought it was St Valentine and we were thrilled.

Birthday parties were held in the Village Hall. Sandwiches, cakes, orange juice, games, balloons and a lot of running about, but all of us on our best behaviour. Although we never travelled on the push and pull train we loved to see it puffing its way through Knapton. After the war when I spent holidays in Knapton I was familiar with all the trains as I travelled from Surrey across London to Liverpool Street then on to Knapton. My bike travelled ahead of me as advanced luggage. The journey home was never as exciting, after six weeks by the seaside. Life was simple healthy happy and straight forward and worry free for us children with lots of innocent fun. Oh happy days....

EDWARD LANGHAM
at Knapton School 1944 to 1945

Knapton school was remarkable in that it only had two rooms, one for the 'infants' and the other for all the rest of the children up to the school leaving age. This meant that Mrs Johnson had to teach at several different levels at the same time. She did this by dividing the class of twenty or so children into several groups and then teaching and giving an assignment to each group in turn, although how she did this and kept order in the whole class defies the imagination.

In the school, on the wall behind her chair and desk, was a large wooden panel with the names of all the children who had passed the eleven plus. That was the entrance examination for grammar school and there must have been twenty or thirty names on it. A remarkable achievement for a one-room village school with only one or two children in that age group each year. Roger Dixon, a boy of my age and a friend at the time, passed this exam and went on to become head boy at the Paston Grammar School (where Nelson had been a pupil). Jill Watts was another very bright young child in the village and, besides entertaining us with her piano playing, she frequently won prizes at the Cromer Music Festival.

Around the school there were three small and separate playgrounds for boys, girls and infants. In addition to providing a play area between lesson times, Mrs Johnson used the playgrounds to teach us country dancing (PT as well probably but I don't remember that). The country dancing sticks in my memory as one of the things of cultural value that I was first introduced to at the Knapton School. Such things instilled in childhood have a way of becoming life values and I think it is no accident that I joined the English Folk Dance and Song Society later on when I was a student at the University of London. I'm sure that the novelty and romance of the country experience must also have been a major factor.

Life in the school house was primitive by modern standards. There was no electricity and, as I mentioned, light was provided by Aladdin or Tilley lamps. In these the fuel pipe had first to be heated with burning alcohol and then, when it was hot enough, paraffin was pumped through and the gas from vaporised paraffin burned over a mantle making it incandescent. Quite a ceremony. A radiation room heater based on a similar system was occasionally used but in winter, most of the time, at the end of the day, a coal fire was lit. In either case this was only in one small room (about 10' x 12') where all six of us had our meals and sat afterwards.

With such a houseful and the school responsibilities, Mrs Johnson had a lady from the village come in to cook the meals. Most of the cooking was done over paraffin wick stoves but, once a week, the range was fired up to make cakes. The water pump in the kitchen was fed by rainwater but though this was soft, and so ideal for washing clothes, it was not drinkable. For that we had an outside pump with its own well. The outdoor toilet was the 'bucket' system and it was emptied once a week by a fellow who came round with a special cart. (At times this might happen while one was sitting there!) The school toilets also had buckets and they were collected the same way.

Once a week we four children had a bath in a tin bath on the floor of the kitchen and we took it in turns to use the same water. (The girls first rule applied so yours truly always ended up bathing in dirty, cold water!) All things considered, although life was simple, we were well off. In particular, unlike the city folk, we were safe and we didn't lack for food.

From our point of view, the stay in Knapton was a big adventure. We children didn't really understand what the war was about, though I do remember Mrs Johnson pointing out the rocket trails to me as the V2s left their launch pads in Holland. (Of course, I also remember the barrage balloons, the dogfights, the bombings and the V1 flying bombs in London but that is another story.)

We could not go on the beach at Mundesley because the cliffs had been mined in anticipation of a German invasion. This was a major problem for many years after the war because the cliffs were being eroded continuously and so many of the mines were lost and buried in the sand.

For children from suburban London, living in the country was magic. It all seemed so alive and exciting. Of course, staying with the school teacher was a big factor and I remember vividly being taken on nature walks where she would point out all kinds of things to us. Almost as fascinating was the way of life of the village people. I remember spending hours watching the blacksmith (whose name I've forgotten), visiting a villager who collected semi-precious stones (Mr Turney?), wandering along farm lanes (lokes) and visiting Uncle Arthur's chicken houses. In retrospect, I think part of the pleasure lay in the sense of community, something that is sadly lacking in urban life. I am sure that all of those early experiences are part of the reason I love the English countryside still and go walking there whenever I visit.

GILLIAN WATTS (SHEPHARD)
at Knapton School 1945 to 1951

My earliest memories are of the Second World War. This is partly because my father served in the Marines, and I have vivid memories of him walking to the station along the footpath that we could see from our back garden. We waved until he went out of sight. He made a dugout shelter in the garden but it was never used. My mother and I used to go to Norwich on the train, to see three of my aunts and their families, who lived there, and who were surviving the air raids on the city. At night the siren would sound and we would all go into the cellar. I can remember the sound of planes and no doubt, doodlebugs. I suppose Knapton was on some kind of flight path from RAF Coltishall to the coast. On occasion, the planes would drop strips of silver paper - I never knew why, but I had the idea that the paper was somehow poisonous. I can remember the huge sense of relief on V.E. Day. A barn dance was held to celebrate in Mr May's barn. We were asked to provide flowers to decorate the barn, and I insisted that we do so. We took down a jam jar filled with marigolds which I thought entirely beautiful. I was mortified to find, when we went down later to see the barn before the dance started, that my offering had been placed behind a beam. The atmosphere was extraordinary, because the barn was huge, dusty from just having been swept, and absolutely full of flowers.

My grandfather, Walter Watts, died suddenly in 1943. He was looking at some bullocks in Wallage's Loke, in a cattle shed a half mile from the farm, when he dropped down dead. My father was there with others, thank goodness, as my grandfather's body had to be carried back to the farm on a hurdle. I remember this, but cannot remember the funeral. My cousin, Philip Almey, can recall the funeral, as he and all the cousins were in our house opposite the church, while the parents went to the service.

Walter Watts, cattle dealer, grandfather of Jill Watts, with his cousin, 'Smock' Watts, drover

I can also remember the General Election in 1945. The result was announced three weeks after the Election, on July 26th. Obviously at five years old, I did not understand what an election was, but what I did know was that the result had caused gloom to engulf our household. My mother and I went out into the village street. People were calling to one another, and saying either 'We've won,' or 'They've won'. When I asked what had happened, my mother said, 'They've got rid of Mr Churchill' I can distinctly recall believing that this must mean that after all, and despite the barn dance, the Germans had won the war, because who else could possibly have got rid of Mr Churchill? It was a great *puzzle* for some time.

My father's family had lived in Knapton for generations. As far back as we can remember, they were cattle dealers who also kept livestock and poultry, on a small scale. Because cattle dealing involved attending cattle markets, they had to have transport, horses and carts at first of course, and then cars very early on. My father had an early Ford (BNG 20). My grandfather's car, which my father inherited, was an Austin (AVF 348). The leather seats smelt strongly when the car was hot, and the roof leaked. The family had a telephone early also. They had a small piece of ground opposite the shop where they kept a few pigs and chickens, but also kept carts and the cars. This was known as the Pightle, and my cousin Brian today lives in a bungalow he built there. The family travelled widely by the standards of the day. My grandfather and father attended markets close at hand, Aylsham on Mondays, Stalham on Tuesdays, Norwich and Bury St Edmunds on Wednesdays, North Walsham on Thursdays, and Norwich again on Saturdays. Once the main business of buying and selling was concluded, participants retired to the pubs. For this reason, Michael and Nancy Miller's father would sometimes accompany my grandfather and father to markets, in order to drive them home! They also occasionally went to Leicester, York and Clonmel in Ireland, buying cattle. On at least one occasion cattle were brought back to Knapton Station. They would then hire land to fatten the cattle before they were resold.

My father was born in a house in Knapton Street. Later on the family, with its six children, moved to Verbena at the bottom of the Street. My grandmother, who had been a lady's maid at Scottow Hall, lived there until her death in 1957. My great aunt Adeline Watts, my grandfather's sister, also lived in the Street, opposite the church, near Roger Dixon and Llewellyn Kirk. She married her cousin, Lew, also Watts, who was I think a drover, but also a fighter and boxer. Lew Watts died in about 1943. My mother and I went to Aunt Adeline's house, where her family, sisters Kaomi, Augusta (Philip Almey's grandmother), and Melvina, and brother Armine, were sitting in appropriate silence. The ladies were wearing hats, which I thought odd, since they were indoors. I felt they needed cheering up, so embarked on a song and dance act which had to be quickly discouraged. My uncle Leslie lived with his wife and children, Brian, Josephine and Patrick, in the Station Loke, next to Neville Coe and his family on one side, and to Billy Small the carpenter, on the other side. Billy Small was married to my grandmother's sister, Virtue. This great aunt was fanatically house proud, and was famous in the family for making her husband shave in the shed.

My mother came from Sheffield. Her parents were wholesale fruiterers. She had come to Mundesley in 1928 to work at the Royal Hotel for her uncle and aunt, Sam and Lily Slater. Uncle Sam had been a prize fighter, and Aunt Lily had, as my mother put it, 'trodden the boards in Blackpool.' My mother did bar and domestic work in the hotel, and while she was there, met my father and married him in Knapton Church in 1932. As a Yorkshire woman, she had a lot in common with Mrs Johnson, also from Yorkshire, and during the war they became friends. This meant that I was brought up very close to Kathleen Johnson, and as a result benefited more than most from Mrs Johnson's influence.

I assume I started school when I was five, in January 1945. I remember going regularly to school before that, on Friday afternoons, and on one occasion, being unable to open the door into the school, or make anyone hear that I was outside. In the end, I very nearly broke the door down in my panic.

When I started school proper, Nancy Miller, Michael's sister used to call for me. We all wore knitted pixie hoods. Nancy's was pale blue angora, which I thought was the last word in prettiness. I can recall making paper chains, and cutting the paper with blunt-ended scissors, I can remember using reading cards with a daisy in the corner, by which you held the card, and writing on small individual boards, with chalk which covered you with dust. We did a play. It must have been a Christmas play, because the words I had to say, which I remember still, were, 'I want a dolly with blue eyes.' I went home for dinner, but on occasions was allowed to stay. The meals were brought from Bacton in a van. I well recall corned beef with grated carrot, and baked potatoes with a large dollop of marge. I also remember an extremely curious purple jelly, which I was convinced was made from methylated spirit, as it was exactly the same colour. School milk put me off milk for life. It was either freezing cold, or warmed up, and always seemed to me either to be very nearly sour, or to taste strongly of whatever the cows had been fed.

Food was very important. During the war, there had been rationing. People were allocated a designated grocer. Ours was Rusts in North

Walsham. I can remember sitting perched on a chair while my mother's purchases were weighed out and the coupons snipped out of our ration books. Sugar came in a twist of blue paper; butter, marge and lard were weighed out and wrapped in greaseproof paper, bacon likewise. There was only one kind of biscuit, a Lincoln biscuit. I thought that they were what biscuits were, a kind of generic term. I had no idea what other kinds might be like. At home, like most people, we had chickens for eggs and for eating. When my father was at home, he used to dress and pack up chickens to be sent by post to our relatives in Sheffield at Christmas. We also kept a few pigs. Every so often one would be killed, butchered, and made into joints, sausages, hams, and delicious pig's fry (the offals). People gave each other meat, eggs, farm butter, in exchange for other goods, or for the same, when their turn came round. Everyone had a garden where fruit and vegetables were grown. Surplus fruit and tomatoes were bottled, or made into jam or chutney. We collected rose hips and acorns – what could the acorns have been for? I can still remember the taste of the war time orange juice, which had to be diluted, and which was provided through the school. It was made using not only the fruit but the rind as well, which gave it a particular tang. Bread of course was not rationed during the war, but was rationed in 1946 to help alleviate famine in Asia, and also in Germany. I can still recall the raised voices of my mother and other women as they stood outside the baker's in Mundesley. 'We came all through the war without this etc.' Really they did have a point. My mother, everyone's mother according to the recollections in this book, performed miracles of cuisine with minimal cooking equipment. Most cooked in an oven in the wall, or on oil stoves, with a tin oven perched on top. Mrs Johnson discovered the pressure cooker almost as soon as they were introduced. With her crammed lifestyle, she benefited enormously from the reduced cooking times it allowed.

When electricity came to Knapton in 1948, it did make cooking easier, although cuts in supply and the cost made many keep faithful to the old oil stove. The electricity engineers and workers invaded the village for a number of weeks. I have a feeling that the foreman, a man named Walter from Ipswich, was billeted on us. He used to bring supplies of fairy cake bought in Sainsburys, in Ipswich, which we found incomparably delicious. When she died at 94, my mother was still using the saucepans she had bought to use on her first electric cooker.

Because food shortages loomed so large in our lives, exceptions to the general austerity rule were memorable. Pamela Dixon's mother put on the most amazing parties in the Shop House. To start with, there would be a fire in the sitting room and the living room as well. We would have games, like Blind Man's Buff and Hunt the Thimble. Then there would be Tea. The table groaned with every kind of sandwich, meat and fish paste, egg, sardine, and every kind of home made cake, jam tarts, maids of honour, iced buns, iced Lincoln biscuits, fruit cake, and there would also be Victoria sponge, jellies, blancmange or 'shape' as it was known, jelly creams with hundreds and thousands on top, and tea or squash to drink. Mrs Dixon also, memorably, provided us with hot cocoa made with milk during the Great Snow of 1947, when we would spend the whole morning playing in the Street, as there was no school.

Many others have described their first banana, or ice cream and the ice cream vans that brought it to the village. Others have mentioned the regular visits to the village of the fish and chip van, belonging to Mr Ward. In 1948, my father's chickens, which were then kept in a field he owned a mile away towards Mundesley, were stolen. I can still remember his rage when he came back to tell us, shouting, 'They've taken the lot.' Obviously we rang the police at once, but there was no breakthrough until Mr Ward remembered seeing a strange lorry in the village a few days earlier. He had noted the number on the inside wall of his van 'just in case.' He had then cleaned the inside walls of his van and with them, the number, but fortunately had committed it to memory. It was indeed the thieves' lorry, and they were traced to the East End of London, living among their stolen haul of birds.

It is hard to disentangle what I remember of Mrs Johnson at Knapton School and what I remember of her as a person and a family friend. She certainly had a number of personal qualities which made her a unique and remarkable teacher. First, she had enthusiasm and an unquenchable interest in learning. She infected all her pupils with her own unbounded interest in learning and new information. She was an unrufflable woman, who sailed through all kinds of vicissitudes, apparently unscathed. She had great confidence, and a great sense of humour. Quite frequently she was overcome by fits of the giggles, although not in working hours. She must also have had boundless energy, because what she packed into a day would have felled a lesser woman.

Not only did she make an incalculable contribution to the education of all those who passed through her hands at Knapton School, she also took a very active part in the life of the village. We see her organising nativity plays, outings and competitions, the National Savings drive, the collection of salvage, running the library service from the school, raising funds for a village playing field, working as a member of the W.V.S., running whist and beetle drives in the village hall – she seemed tireless.

Of course, others were also involved in running the village. The parish council, the School Managers, the Parochial Church Council, had a number of individuals who were prominent in all three. Miss Robinson, and her companion, Miss Leather, were really ever present and all powerful, but in an entirely benign way. Miss Robinson visited the sick – she brought a selection of Victorian children's books for me to read once when I was confined to bed with a mastoid for three weeks. She gave Christmas presents to the whole of the village. Major and later Mrs Wilkinson served tirelessly on council and committees. Mr May, at Church Farm and later Mrs May were very free with their time and energy in public work in the village. Henry Wild, father of June Wild was a parish councillor for almost the whole of his life and secretary to many committees. Bob and Grace Wright gave dancing lessons. Mr and Mrs Hicks, and Ursula Fawkes were not only heavily involved in the Chapel, but ran youth groups as well. There was always something that needed a money raising effort, and almost everyone contributed to running whist drives, dances, socials, fêtes and so on.

The influence of the Chapel was, it seems to me, greater on children and young people in the village than that of the church. The Chapel had a large Sunday School and a Youth Group called Christian Endeavour, which had all kinds of activities, competitions and outings, and made a real contribution to all our lives, regardless of whether we were chapel or church goers. The church also had a Sunday School but it attracted younger children. It did run an annual outing to Great Yarmouth on the train. The main feature of this was lunch in a café, followed by an afternoon at the Pleasure Beach. We enjoyed it, but it could not be said to be as thrilling as the London and Blakeney Point trips we took from school.

Even as a child, I was conscious that Mrs Johnson was somewhat in awe of The Office, as the Education Committee offices were known. She frequently mentioned the names of the Primary School Education Officer, and the Chief Education Officer. The Office was in charge of supplies to the school, and each autumn a huge case arrived, containing the Requisition, exercise and text books, pencils, pens, crayons, paint and ink, and materials for craft, sewing and knitting. It was hugely exciting to help unpack all these interesting things, and to speculate about the lessons which would ensue.

Looking back, I think that those who enjoyed school during Mrs Johnson's time were, more than anything, enthused by her style of teaching. The Eleven Plus was a great divide. For a year before the exam, we were given homework in English, Arithmetic and what was known as

Knapton School Sports Team 1947

From left to right: Shirley Wright, Yvonne Lee, Janet Woolsey (behind),
Betty Wright, Avril Edwards, Jill Watts, Barbara Dixon (behind Jill),
Pamela Dixon (behind Barbara), Brian Puncher, Michael Miller,
Russell Woolsey (behind Michael), Tommy Rose, Brian Watling,
Willie Puncher, Kathleen Johnson (behind Willie), Brian Eastoe,
John Rayner, Derek Miller

Intelligence. Our work was corrected by Mrs Johnson and a creditable number of us went through to the grammar schools in North Walsham. But others did not, and the bitter disappointment caused by the so-called failure is vividly described by Shirley Wright (now Conquest) and by John Rayner. On the day I was to take the Scholarship, I got measles, and so did Margaret Wild, who was due to take it as well. We had to take it again when we were better. Anne Lee (now Isitt) describes how she was sick with nerves at having to go to Mundesley School to take the exam, and had to take it later, but at Knapton, and passed. And so did I, and what happened next is another story.

PAMELA DIXON (GARNHAM)
at Knapton School 1946 to 1949

I remember Mrs Johnson, Mr Featherstone, Mrs Featherstone, Miss Collier, and of course, Miss Townsend (my aunt). I remember the school dentist with dread as I had bad teeth, and also the nit nurse, and little bottles of milk which when frozen on frosty days were put on the fireguard to thaw. I walked to school as it was only a few minutes. I remember Sports Day at North Walsham School. I usually did high jump and long jump. We did country dancing in the playground to the wind-up gramophone.

The Men's Club was nicknamed 'The Cup of Tea Boys.' In my teens I joined the Chapel Youth Group and as a child belonged to the Girls' Life Brigade which was based at Mundesley. Before electricity we had a tin oven set over two oil stoves. Water came to Knapton in 1957, I think at the end of October.

Village events often took place on the meadow opposite Knapton Hall, now called Lawn Close.

Arthur Fincham, uncle of Pamela and Barbara Dixon, getting water from his well

I had my first banana during the war. My cousin was in the Navy and brought some back when he came on leave. When I lived at Paston, ice creams came to the shop once a month. I remember standing on the bank opposite our house watching for the van to arrive. They were all sold in half an hour. There were Lyons ice creams, round, with paper around them and pink or white. During the war, my mother used to mix some cheese in a thick batter and fry it. It was our Saturday treat. At the end of sweet rationing, I got hazlenut creams as my first sweets.

In the snow in 1947, I walked down Mundesley Road. The snow towered above both sides of the road. We had to walk to get milk from the farms in Hall Lane.

I remember the village hall dances and socials with Grace and Bob Wright and later with Joyce and Bob Crisp of Crisp's Taxis. They would hold dances in different village halls and we would cycle to them all, Gimingham, Trunch and so on. I also remember going to Grace and Bob Wright's for sing-songs round the piano. I used to play the piano, not very well I think. There used to be 8 or 10 of us, and there was always plenty of food to eat.

I belonged to the chapel youth group. We always did a Christmas play and a concert after the Whit Monday fête. Mr Waller from North Walsham and Michael Hicks used to organise us.

BARBARA DIXON (JARVIS)
at Knapton School 1946 to 1952

Things I remember of Knapton and Paston.

At the age of six I was dropped off a bus at Paston village hall. I was an evacuee from London. I was taken in by Mr and Mrs Dixon and Miss Townsend (later dinner lady) who lived with the Dixons as the two ladies were sisters.

The first thing I needed to do was to spend a penny (remember I had just left London with electric lights and flush toilets). I was taken down the garden with a torch to sit on a wooden seat over a bucket. Squares of newspaper cut and tied hung on the wall if you needed it; that was a bit of a shock.

I remember going to a court aged 8 to be adopted, not too certain what it meant, but I was told I had to forget London and the people as I belonged to Norfolk now.

We moved to Knapton when I was 8. Dad Dixon bought the shop; we also had the Post Office; he also had a lot of poultry. Gillian lived with her Mum and Dad just across the road. I was always made very welcome at their home. Janet Steward lived at the back of our house and we used to call each other from our bedroom windows.

I remember the big room at Knapton School, also Mrs Johnson and Mrs Featherstone.

When the King died I remember Mrs Johnson turning the radio up (wireless) so we could all hear it as they announced Princess Elizabeth would now be Queen.

Yes, I picked pinks and tied them into bunches – couldn't think why they were called pinks as they were white. I don't know what we did with them after they were cut.

Mrs Johnson would take the gramophone into the playground; we did lots of country dancing which I loved. She would also do PT with us outside.

The Dentist van would come every 6 months and park just outside the school gate. I was one of the first to go (anything to get out of a lesson, not very smart).

We always sat at the same desk and near Mrs Johnson's desk was a lovely coal fire with a big guard around.

I believe also we had a small fish tank with goldfish on the window sill.

I always looked forward to my little bottle of milk.

The sports days were really exciting, going to North Walsham.

I left Knapton School when I was 14 and went to North Walsham for one year.

After I left school I worked for Dad Dixon at home. I had to collect the newspapers from the railway station each day, sort them and then deliver round the village on a bicycle with two big bags. The rest of the day collect and wash the chickens eggs.

I always went to church and Sunday school every Sunday morning but when I was 11 I started to go to the little Methodist Chapel as well. After the service Mr and Mrs Hicks (affectionately know to us youngsters as 'Marney and Dimps') gave us a welcome to their home. Marnie would make tea and cakes etc. and we became one big family. We also used to meet at their home on Wednesday evenings for a Youth Fellowship meeting which lasted one hour. We would always sing a hymn, say a prayer and Dimps talked to us about the Bible. We could always ask questions and discuss things we didn't understand. After the meeting, out came the tea and cakes etc. There were sometimes as many as 12-15 of us – we must have eaten them out. But getting together each week taught us how to share and be kind and thoughtful to each other.

The Fellowship had a fête every Whit Monday at Mrs May's farm. We all ran stalls, made the teas etc. and then in the evening we performed a concert in the village hall, very tired but happy.

Just before each Christmas we performed a Nativity play also in the village hall.

❧

JOHN WRIGHT
at Knapton School 1946 to 1955

John started school in 1946. His teachers were Mrs Johnson, Mrs Featherstone, and Mrs Spurgeon coming to teach when there was illness. He had school dinners, the meals came from Bacton and Miss Townsend was the dinner lady.

Mr Jack Leeder came each year to judge the garden plots which had been worked in pairs. On Thursdays, the boys went to Southrepps school by coach for woodwork lessons. During the winter months, if the weather was bad, they were picked up earlier from Southrepps and taken home a different way if the snow had blocked the roads. Boys also went from Ashmanaugh and Bacton. The lessons were held in a hut and Mr Strong was the teacher. They had lunch in the canteen and played on the common afterwards.

On school trips they went by coach to London (the younger ones went to Blakeney) and visited St Paul's Cathedral, the Tower of London, Madame Tussaud's and always ended up at the Zoo. On one trip they had to go to Scotland Yard to pick up, he thinks, Margaret Self, who had got lost. On another trip, John remembers standing on scaffolding outside Buckingham Palace to watch the Queen come out on to the balcony.

Playtimes at school were spent on the field opposite the village hall. John remembers the new playing field (next to the Men's Club) being prepared by John Grey, and the building of the water tower, the council houses and bungalows in School Close when he biked to school.

When school finished, the boys met on the cross roads by Harry Sexton's house (John's great uncle) to play football, not many cars about then.

He remembers being on Guyton's Farm pulling wild oats and learning to drive on the fields. For a while he did bell-ringing in the church, and on Tuesdays it was Christian Endeavour at the chapel.

John had his own chickens which he looked after, and he had enough eggs to send to the egg packing station at North Walsham where his sister Betty worked.

When he was 14 in 1955, John went to the Secondary Modern School in North Walsham.

BRIAN WILD
at Knapton School 1946 to 1955

I went to Knapton School at the age of five until I was fourteen. I can remember doing dancing, cricket, and gardening. We went on outings to Blakeney Point to see the nesting terns with Ted Eales and on trips to London, where we went to the Zoo, and on the River Thames.

On Thursdays, I went to Southrepps and Antingham School for woodwork. It was in a long wooden hut in the playground. We had a hot meal in the canteen and afterwards we went on the common to play, and sometimes to the shop for sweets. We went on a Starlings bus, and picked up boys from other schools.

When I left Knapton School I went to North Walsham Secondary School My form teacher was Mr Cork who also taught metal work and English. He was very kind to me. I was in Cavell House.

When I left school I got a job as a gardener in Mundesley on Paston Road. I stayed there a short time and then got a job in Knapton in Pond Road as a gardener. It was 5 days a week 10 a.m. to noon.

I also took over the paper round in Knapton from the Dixon family who kept the shop. I had to go to Knapton Station to collect papers and magazines at about 7.30 a.m. It was half a mile's bike ride. I would sort them out on the kitchen table before taking them round. It would take me about 2 hours to go round, all weathers. Some people would moan if their papers got wet or I was late. I would collect the money on Saturday mornings. I sometimes had to walk round when the roads were icy or blocked with snow. I had one or two people made me cups of tea. I also got bitten by dogs several times. I finished doing the papers after about 40 years. They gave me a party and presented me with a certificate and a medal which was a nice thought.

To fill up my time I did work on Mr Cargill's Farm pulling wild oats and picking broad beans. I also helped Arthur Claydon carting sugar beet to Knapton Station and loading trucks. I also helped on Mr Guyton's White House Farm collecting sugar beet tops for cattle feed.

JOHN RAYNER
at Knapton School 1946 to 1950

Before Knapton (1936-1945)
I was born on March 12 1936 in Briggate, Worstead. My father was a painter and glazier so his income was limited. Fortunately during the depression my father was lucky to have had some work. Also, although we certainly had no luxuries, we seemed to eat reasonably well. My father grew lots of vegetables in the garden. I started school at Honing.

A particularly memorable event was being in Jenny Lind hospital, at Unthank and Colman Roads in Norwich, to have my tonsils and adenoids out.

Whilst I was there, patients were taken into a basement or hallway during an air raid. I was very cold and, most likely as a result, caught some illness which led to a long convalescence. Between July 1940 and August 1941 there were 29 raids on the city of 126,000 people. In 1942 the centre of Norwich was obliterated.

World War II began in September 1939. My father was conscripted into the army in March 1941. At about that time my parents bought a house on Trunch Road in Mundesley near my father's former employer, Bertie Gotts, the builder. The house had running cold water and a flush toilet. My mother and I moved there and I went to Mundesley school which was 100 yards down road to the east from where we lived. I was not particularly happy there. The teacher seemed to pick on me and I had trouble with a neighbourhood bully.

While we were living in Mundesley the Germans bombed the area. They were probably trying to hit the military targets of the holiday camp and the sanatorium where soldiers were billeted. They would drop flares first and the whole night sky was lit up like the daytime. Fortunately no buildings were hit although windows were blown out in some houses (not ours). The bombs produced a row of craters in the fields behind our house and I used to search them for shrapnel. Since we had no shelter, during the air raids my mother and I would go next door (attached bungalow) to sleep with Mrs Buck and daughter, Sandra, in their inside steel shelter. I could only just sit up in it. It was composed of a flat steel plate on legs and called a Morrison shelter. Another kind of shelter, the Anderson, was of corrugated metal and shaped like an upside down U buried in the ground outside. We later had one of these at ground level for a shed.

After a few months my mother took me to live with her parents in East Ruston. I returned to Honing school instead of going to the nearer East Ruston School.

Each weekend my grandfather (and sometimes I) poached for pheasant or rabbit on East Ruston Commons. He had a jacket with inside pockets that took the double barrels of the 12-bore on one side and the butt on the other.

There was also sufficient room for the catch. I would help him set snares for rabbits. This meant that we always had plenty of meat during that war rationing period. Our garden was fairly large and grandfather grew most vegetables. He also raised chickens and rabbits. We had a dog and a cat and at one period a goat which was milked. That milk tasted differently from cows milk and I don't think I liked it very much. Like Briggate the toilet was in a building in the garden, water came from a well, and heating came from one stove. My grandmother would make our bread and I used to knead the dough which was allowed to rise in front of the open fire. It was cooked in an oven in the wall.

Our clothes were aired (dried) on wooden horses in front of the fire. They were checked for moisture content by placing them on a mirror (cold) on the wall for evidence of fogging. We may have had another fireplace in the front room. For lighting we relied on oil lamps and candles. (I still have the brass candle holder I used to take to bed with me.) It was a great advance when my grandparents purchased a pressurized lamp. It was so bright!

My grandfather came from Happisburgh and had several brothers and sisters though we saw them seldom. I recall the story that he had run away to sea when he was 12. I believe he served in the merchant navy but he was in the Royal Navy and also went trawling. We often had fish to eat, especially fresh herring and kippers. The latter are smoked herring with all their bones which were fairly difficult to remove when they were eaten. My grandfather also drove a traction engine and I can recollect going to a farm just down the road to the east of Honing school to collect sheaves with horse-drawn wagons. The traction engine powered the threshing machine with a belt. One of the farm workers was an Italian prisoner of war. My grandfather always treated me well and often took me with him, and as far as I can remember now, never scolded me. He had severe asthma. In a shed he kept all kinds of tools in old cooking pans and bits and pieces of 'junk'. I now have a similar collection.

My grandmother spoiled me and, although she couldn't have had very much, always gave me money even up to the time I went to university. My mother was her only child and therefore I was her only

John Rayner's great grandfather driving a traction engine.
His grandfather drove a similar one.

grandchild. She bought me the 'racing' bike (i.e. drop handlebars), that I had always wanted, when I was in my teens. I used to ride it up to S.W. London to visit Kathleen Johnson's friends, Edward and Josephine Langham. I was particularly proud of the record of once completing that 141.3 mile trip in 13 hours and 25 minutes with stops (average of 10.53 m.p.h.). In 1952 Edward and I cycled 1290 miles to Land's End and back.

Although my mother had worked in a clothing store in North Walsham before she was married I don't think she ever had a regular job after I was born.

She must have depended upon my father's army pay and her parents. However, I don't remember wanting much although I always longed for an electric train set like the one I used to feast my eyes upon in Langley's window in the arcade in Norwich. Much later in the 1970s I bought myself an engine there.

During this period of my life I amused myself much of the time roaming the commons by myself. The commons were open common land covered with gorse and occupied several separate sections of the village. People would dig for sand in some areas and also dump rubbish there. I did not read. I probably couldn't read very well anyway.

One thing I liked to do, and which I continued into my adult life, was to draw maps of the local area and copies of areas of the world. There was no one to play with of my age that I knew in East Ruston as I did not go to East Ruston school to meet the locals. I do not recall being unhappy.

We walked a lot and for farther distances went by bicycle. My family never had a car while I lived at home. Petrol was severely rationed during the War and we probably could not have used a car anyway. We went most often to North Walsham, to see my paternal grandparents and cousins and not to the nearer Stalham. Occasionally we went on a bus to Norwich and less frequently to Great Yarmouth. It was in Great Yarmouth, I believe in the autumn, that we used to watch the herring fleet come in and the visiting Scottish women gut the fish at a fantastic rate.

My mother did read to me and it seems that I learned to listen and absorb.

At Briggate she would read out the newspaper strip about Rupert the Bear. At East Ruston she would read from 'The Children's Friend' magazine. (Aitken, W. Francis [ed.], 1913: *The Children's Friend and Play-hour Companion*. Vol. LII. Annual for 1913 containing parts for 1912. S.W. Partridge & Co., Ltd., London). This was probably hers from her childhood as she was born in 1912. In particular I was enthralled by the story 'The Splendid Stars' (Bone, Florence). Later she read *The Magic Garden* to me. (Stratton-Porter, Gene, 1927: *The Magic Garden*. Greycaine Book Manufacturing Company Limited, Watford, U.K.) As I learned very much later Stratton-Porter was an American feminist, environmentalist, photographer, and one of Indiana's most famous female authors.

I think it might have been during this period that a ship carrying a cargo of oranges got into trouble or sank and many many crates were washed up on shore. Oranges were quite scarce and probably expensive so we went down to the beach and eagerly collected bags of them.

What went on in the war was mainly beyond my real comprehension. I remember pictures in the paper, newsreels at the cinema, adults talking about it, and the bombing in Norwich and in Mundesley. Obviously my father was away. We saw him when he came home on leave and we visited him at least twice in Hastings on the south coast where he was stationed with the searchlights and big guns. In 1941 I caught whooping cough there and we had to stay for an extended period of time. We visited caves in the city where people were living for safety from air-raids. Once my father came home for 'special' leave.

My mother was very upset. This must have been for D-Day (June 6th 1944) because my father went to Normandy that day. I believe my father was injured once by flying shrapnel in the ankle but otherwise he escaped unharmed. On reflection though, he must have been traumatized by the carnage he saw as he would later talk in anguish to my mother about it.

The period has been documented in many books and films. Clearly people suffered a great deal both directly through losing loved ones and having very limited resources. Nevertheless people put up with it (British stiff upper lip!) and seemed to enjoy life. Loyalty to the crown and country was very strong.

There was great affection and respect for the Royal Family during this dreadful period and, I believe, this accounts for the continuing support for Queen Elizabeth II from some sections of the population as we move into the 21st century.

When Germany capitulated in 1945 we had a local celebration in the village – V.E. Day. A big bonfire, composed in part of old tyres, was set near East Ruston school. I was smacked hard by my mother for running in and out of the very black smoke.

Knapton (1946-1950)

With the return of my father in January 1946 we moved back to Mundesley.

My mother was aware of my problems at the local school during our first stay in Mundesley, so she arranged for me to go to the school in the next village, Knapton. I rode my bike, about 1.5 miles and may have gone home for lunch some days. I believe lunch used to arrive already cooked possibly in North Walsham, by a car or lorry (?).

Although I was nicknamed 'Cranky' it seemed in the end to be a term of endearment rather than a slur. I have no idea how I got it. Early on some of the bigger bully boys may have given it to me. I remember being beaten up and lying on the floor of the boys toilet which stank. Things changed as I grew older and I remember that I began to dominate the football games we played with a tennis ball in the southern-most school yard at breaks.

Knapton school was small, only two main rooms. The younger children (under 8?) were in one room and the older (8-14) were in another. Mrs Kathleen (Kitty) Johnson was the teacher of the older group and lived in the school house next door with her husband Arthur and daughter Kathleen. Somehow she managed to teach this wide range of students. There must have been 20 or so in the main room. The pupils would start out in the front row when they were young and then move back as they grew older.

105

Late on Friday(?) afternoons we had a period when we had to write down all the possible arithmetic and calendar relationships we could remember by heart. I enjoyed it and learned all my multiplication tables that way. It seems to me I wrote fast and got everything down I knew each week. I also did well on intelligence tests. I do not think that my learning of English and spelling went as well. However, the half dozen notebooks I still have from the 1946-49 period show me writing quite well with only a few blotches from the pen dipped in ink.

One thing I particularly liked was the period when Mrs Johnson would read to us. The books were written by authors such as Malcolm Saville and Arthur Ransome and their words still resonate today. I enjoyed handwork like drawing and painting and we had various projects such as making Christmas trimmings. We would also pick flowers and then bring them to the classroom to draw them. At some point we went in for a competition to paint the Union Jack (U.K. flag) for the National Savings Week. I won 1st Prize from the Smallburgh Committee.

I liked gardening and pairs of us, one older and one younger boy only, were each assigned plots of our own to look after. Arthur Johnson helped supervise. I suspect that the girls did cooking and sewing with Mrs Johnson at those times. We were awarded prizes for our efforts and I believe I was given several. One flower which did well in the general garden was the 'pink', a white carnation. We sold these and the money went to pay for our trips. We must have done other things too to collect money such as running whist drives. These trips were wonderful. The younger children went on a bus ride to Cromer. I went on that once so I was possibly in the younger room in 1946. I do not remember the teacher although the names Breeze and Featherstone seem familiar. Thereafter we went to London by coach. We left at about 6.30 a.m. and went via Newmarket where we had a rest stop. In that town we would see lots of horses being exercised because this was one of the major racing sites in Britain. The horse region of Kentucky reminds me of this area. In London we got around by walking and by using the tube. I'm not certain whether there were other adults but Mr and Mrs Johnson did a magnificent job of shepherding this motley crew around.

They were certainly to be admired for their initiative and patience. They never lost anyone. We might each have had partners to keep an eye on each other.

Each year we went to different places: St Paul's, Westminster Abbey, Madame Tussaud's etc., but we always ended up at Regent's Park Zoo.

We arrived home by midnight. These were certainly most enjoyable and educational outings.

On January 21 1947 we had a tremendous snow storm. Drifts covered the roads and we were cut off for several days from the surrounding villages. Men with shovels eventually cleared the roads around Mundesley. The last snow did not melt that year until April. In a normal year we would get none.

I started playing football for a team, Trunch Rovers, and was playing in 1948 when I was 12. At least one line-up was:

J.Reynolds
K.Stebbings J.Clark
P.Hicks J.Dixon J.Hicks
C.Cutting D.Flaxman M.Dixon J.Rayner P.Bright

One newspaper report indicates that on February 28 1948 I scored two goals in a 3-3 tie with Gimingham.

Knapton, like other schools, participated in sports competitions at North Walsham. The front cover of this book shows our 1949 team.

I also joined Trunch Church choir. I can't think why. The football coach was a Methodist and I don't think I could sing in tune even though I went to lessons by the young organist who lived in North Walsham.

My mother had an organ and later a piano which she would play from time to time. Neighbours used to like to come of an evening to sing to my mother's playing. I enjoyed these happy times. My mother tried to teach me to play but I had insufficient motivation and unfortunately dropped it. I have wished all my life that I had kept it up so I could play an instrument now. I often wonder whether, had I done that, I would have developed a better ear.

In 1948 I was also keeping and rearing rabbits by mating them with Mr Buck's, our neighbour, buck. In March I entered one in a show and won third prize. I had bantams and raised some chicks from eggs. I also spent time collecting car licence plate numbers. In those days there were so few!

In the spring thousands of primroses grew wild along the Trunch Road west of where we lived and we would go picking them. In the summer I would go with my mother to pick blackcurrants in Trunch. We would be paid by the basketful.

We lived only a mile from the beach so I went there often. Somehow in that relatively rough sea I taught myself to swim but I can't remember how old I was. Before that on a number of occasions I would wade in the lows (water filled depressions in the sand at low tide) that in places were deeper than my height. I often think I must have been lucky I did not drown.

One place I did not go on the beach was west of Mundesley to Trimingham.

It was here that mines had been laid in the cliffs during the war. Erosion continually brought the cliff down and the locations of the mines were lost. As a result a permanent bomb disposal unit was stationed there. Even so, over the years several people were killed by the mines.

In England at that time children took a national examination at age 11 known as the '11+' (eleven plus). Depending upon the outcome, the children were divided into those who would go to grammar school and those who would not. Typically the boys went to Paston Grammar School and the girls went to the Girls High, both in North Walsham, where they would learn languages and science, etc. Paston Grammar was where Lord Nelson went to school. In 1947 I failed the 11+. I was very upset about it but upon reflection this outcome was reasonable. I don't think I knew English very well. As a result I stayed at Knapton until I was 14.

One event I remember was the installation of electricity in Knapton. We watched in fascination the digging of holes, erection of poles and the stringing of wires. Some of the men even walked across the road on one wire while holding on to another. It must have made a big difference for the inhabitants. Mundesley already had electricity and gas, by which my mother cooked. However, I had previously had the experience of no public utilities in Briggate and East Ruston.

Mrs Johnson at Knapton School was a very welfare-oriented person. Just after the War she decided we should help children in Germany through the Red Cross. She had us collect things and she sent them to a school in Rodenberg near Hanover. Why that school I do not know, unless it was selected by the Red Cross. Then one of the boys at that school, Walter Peters, wrote to me (probably because I was the one closest to his age). The problem was that his letter was in German. Mrs Johnson told me about a lady, Miss Montford, in Knapton who knew German. As a result I went to ask her to translate the letter. Subsequently she translated more letters from Walter and mine to him.

Miss Montford was a remarkable woman. The daughter of a clergyman, she had an outwardly stern appearance but she was very kind. She was well-educated. I think she had a degree from Cambridge(?), possibly in geography, unusual for a woman of her era. She had been English governess to the German Kaiser's children in the early 1900s and during the First World War was a nurse in Egypt. Her fingers had huge cracks in

Miss Montford

them and she told me it was due to the way they had to disinfected them. The nurses would plunge their hands into boiling water. The very dry air, of course, would remove all the natural oils! She never married. Her house, a bungalow which was called 'Ecclesburn', is just north on the opposite side of the road from the school. Her cousin, Major F. B. Wilkinson, lived on Mundesley Road in Knapton.

After translating a few letters she asked me whether I would like to learn some German. Fool that I was, I said, 'Yes.' That was the beginning of a very good relationship with her and resulted in my further education and what success I made of my life. She said that I had to go before school at 7:30 so I used to cycle to Knapton early those days. After about six weeks she said that since I clearly wanted to learn I could go after school. She was testing me!

I worked in her garden in return for her lessons. Once on a Good Friday she said she didn't think I should be gardening on that day. I told her I saw no reason not to because my father had always had to work on religious holidays and she said no more (probably thought about it though). My family were not church-going and I do not remember why earlier I had started going to Trunch Church. Certainly Miss Montford encouraged me to go to Knapton Church where I was introduced to Revd Thur, an Austrian emigré. He had the two parishes of Knapton and Paston and lived in Paston. He alternated services.

At some point probably in 1952 or 53 until 1955 I became a Sunday School teacher at Paston.

In order to teach me German Miss Montford first had to teach me good English. We read Shakespeare together and went to see his plays at the Maddermarket in Norwich. Later she taught me French and some Latin. She asked me to call her 'Aunt Isabel' and I wrote to her frequently after I left Mundesley until the early 1970s. In 1975 I visited her in a nursing home, Rose Meadow, in North Walsham. She did not know me. She died on 14 September 1984 at the age of 95.

In 1950 Walter Peters became ill with diphtheria and scarlet fever. For convalescence Mrs Johnson organized a drive to collect money to bring him to Norfolk. He stayed with me. The next year I visited Walter in Rodenberg.

Walter Peters at Knapton School 1950
Back Row: Robin Yaxley, Brian Castoe, John Wild, Russell Woolsey, Shirley Wright, Barbara Dixon, Janet Woolsey, Betty Wright, Avril Edwards.
Front Row: Brenda Wilkins, Yvonne Lee, John Wright, John Rayner, Mrs Johnson, Walter Peters, Margaret Wild, Jill Watts, Desmond Hooker.

Subsequent Schooling 1950 - 1955

In the late 1940s the British Government increased the school-leaving age from 14 to 15. As a result, instead of leaving school at Easter in 1950, I had to go to North Walsham Secondary Modern School for a year. There I even had a teacher who had taught my father. I don't remember academic classes very well but I did write a geographical essay, 'My trip around the world,' over several months in 1951 for a Mr Young. (I still have it.) Considering my education to that point I think it was quite good. Clearly working with Miss Montford had helped me enormously so I had gained a reasonable vocabulary and could put a narrative together. Also, I did well at woodwork and metalwork. A beaten copper dish and a small pine cupboard I still have but a larger mahogany bookcase is gone. For some of this work I received a Hobbies Prize on July 11 1951. At home I was doing photographic development. An uncle had shown me how to do it and I set up a dark room in our bathroom. In 1951 I was also doing some electrical wiring for the Gotts firm.

I captained North Walsham School's cricket team and I also played for Paston's village team. During this period I continued work with Miss Montford and attended Knapton Church. I also joined in some Knapton functions.

Nativity Play at the Village Hall
Left to right: John Wild, Barbara Dixon, Shirley Wright, Jessie Rose, Ruth Steward, Mr Hicks, Dorothy Chamberlain

In April 1951 when I was about to leave school my father had arranged for me to have an apprenticeship at the Mundesley Gas Works. However, Miss Montford and probably Mrs Johnson had other ideas. (Unfortunately I do not know the details here or their later involvement in Norwich City College. Stupidly I never asked either Miss Montford or Mrs Johnson.) An interview for me was arranged with a Major Russell, Miss Montford's acquaintance, who ran a private school in Bacton. He boarded and tutored boys from Paston Grammar School who wanted to get into the Dartmouth Naval Academy. He accepted me. The fees must have been quite high and I know that my parents could not have afforded it. I'm surprised they apparently put up no opposition to me going. I can only believe that Miss Montford paid(?). Major Russell also schooled others such as myself. Another boy was Roy Bradbury, son of the teacher at Edingthorpe School. He later married my cousin, Gwen Roberts of North Walsham. Lessons started after the bus brought the grammar school boys home and went on until about 9 p.m. including a period for dinner. In the next six months Major Russell taught me the rudiments of algebra that were to stand me in good stead for the rest of my life. Obviously he gave me this knowledge in just the right form and at a time when I was interested and ready to learn.

Unfortunately in December 1951 Major Russell became ill with malaria, that he had picked up in India, and had to give up. I was out in the cold. This time it was probably Mrs Johnson who got me an interview with Lincoln Ralphs of the Norfolk Education Committee. He sent me to see Olive Browning at Norwich City College (NCC). She had started an unusual programme of training students, who had failed the 11+, to take the O-level examinations. She admitted me!

I started in January 1952. My days were long. Typically I was taking the 7:26 train to Norwich and returning on the 5:18. At least two nights I was taking evening classes and did not get home until 10:30 p.m. Despite the long hours I found the days very enjoyable. I was learning a lot. A letter from Major Russell encouraged me to read good books and newspapers, not use American slang, and to ask questions without pestering. I now planned to be a teacher. In 1953 after 18 months at NCC I took 6 exams at the O (Ordinary) level General Certificate of Education. I did so well that Miss Browning encouraged me to go on the Advanced Level. I took those exams in maths, geography, and history in 1955. I was awarded a County Major Scholarship which paid my way to the University of Birmingham to read Geography.

The storm of early 1953 stands out in my memory. On January 31, 1953 I was at the Oaks dance hall, North Walsham, with my mother and friends for Olde Tyme dancing when we had a very bad gale. Afterwards there were no buses so we had to go home in an RAF truck. The wind had affected the waves in the sea which caused enormous amounts of erosion. On February 1st I went with my neighbour, Mr Buck, in his car to see the 'undescribable' (sic) damage to the coastline, road and houses at Walcot and Bacton. The next day I rode my bicycle to Walcot to see the damage and photograph it.

On the 7th February I went with Mrs Johnson, John Wild and Kathleen to Sea Palling where we filled about 200 sandbags to support the sea wall.

In the 21st century news of natural disasters and human activities are seen in real time on television or through the internet. In the 1940s and

50s it sometimes took several days for photographs to appear in a weekly paper such as the *Norfolk Chronicle*. Television existed but there was very little local coverage. We always had a radio but my family did not have a television until I left home. I did not own one until 1966.

JACKIE CROXON (ELVIN)
at Knapton School 1948 to 1952

I remember
  – the big clock in the Big Room. I was terrified of it. If Mrs Johnson wasn't wearing her watch she would send someone in towards the end of playtime to see what the time was. I couldn't tell the time and would dread that she would send me. I used to drag poor Ruthie Steward in with me so she could tell me what the time was. If she wouldn't come I would make it up and I never got found out.
  – not very much about the Little Room except that when Rodney Edwards started school the door between the little and big room had to be left open or he would cry 'I want my Abby' until it was opened again.
  – the double desks in the Big Room. I sat in front of William (Bibby) Plant and would never dare look at him in the summer as he suffered dreadfully from hay-fever and I knew that if I looked at him my nose and eyes would run in sympathy.
  – that the cloakroom floors were made of concrete and always seemed to be damp.
  – the wind-up gramophone for country dancing, that the girls all loved and the boys all hated, Strip the Willow and the Dashing White Sergeant.
  – the lawn surrounded by the flower beds where we were allowed to sit sometimes in the summer. There was a very pretty tree in the corner. Was it a red hawthorn?
  – Mrs Johnson. How did she manage to teach so many children of different ages so many different subjects all at the same time? She always appeared to be quite calm and fair in her dealings with us. We must have driven her mad!
  – when we passed the 'Scholarship' Mrs Johnson took us (Ruthie Steward, Malcolm Wild and myself, I don't remember if Janet came) for a boat trip on the Broads. A little rowing boat, no life-jackets, we hit Wroxham Bridge, and a picnic of big chunks of bread (that she'd just bought) with butter and raspberry jam. We had a wonderful time. When

we left the school to start at North Walsham she gave us each a present. Mine was *The Observers Book of Wildflowers*.

– once when Cinny and I were in Mundesley Mrs Johnson asked us if we would like to go to Cromer with her as she had to pick Kathleen up from the skating rink. The seats in her car were very slippery and we bounced about all the way there and back. We had our first pomfret cakes that day, I hated them, Cinny loved them.

– I loved Miss Collier. She wore smoky glasses and rode a sit-up-and-beg bike. When I was ill with tonsillitis she made me some blackcurrant jellies in pretty glass dishes.

– Miss Townsend. She was a little round lady in a white overall who for some reason collected brown paper and string. She would fold the paper very carefully and put it in her overall pocket.

– that we had film shows. The films came by post in little silver coloured containers. Mrs Johnson would always use the same envelope to return them and the next lot would again come in the same envelope. She said they were trying to see how many times they could use it.

– learning to knit by knitting a pixie hood. Mine started out as a *very* fetching shade of pale blue but finished up a rather grubby grey. Poor Ruthie found knitting hard and her hood was so full of holes that we called it fishing net. (Cruel!)

– sewing a dress. It was very exciting choosing the material from samples. The style was called Magyar which meant it was two pieces, back and front and we sewed them together. I was very proud of mine and wore it to school. As I reached up to get a book from the library cupboard my beloved dress split all the way down one side.

– mercury in a brown jar that we would pour onto a plate and poke with our fingers to make it form into balls.

– in the scholarship writing about cows. Mrs Watts made us coffee with all milk at break time. There in the bottom of my cup was the milk bottle top. They said it would bring me luck, which it did.

– being very excited when the library van came. We got to choose the books. Wonderful.

– making Christmas decorations. Paper chains which had to be glued and strange paper lanterns. There was a charity poster of a Christmas tree full of presents. If you took a penny(?) you got to put your name on a present. I was not at all interested in the charity as long as I could get my name on that yellow balloon. I loved stencilling cards, bashing away with those stiff little brushes.

– that we had a carol concert and mums and dads came. My mum bought me some real lisle stockings for the occasion. They were held up with elastic garters. I was in the front row facing the audience, singing as well as I could, when I happened to look down. My beautiful stockings were in a puddle round my ankles. Oh the shame of it.

– I enjoyed school dinners but I hated the milk. In the winter it was warmed up and always tasted of fish.

– gardening. It always seemed to be sunny when we did the gardens and we all seemed to enjoy it. My favourite job was hoeing the gravel at the front of the school.

– walking to school with my sister (Cinny). We never seemed to hurry but I don't remember ever being late. Certain rituals had to be observed on the way. First we had to touch the snake. This was a thick, twisted ivy stem growing in the hedge between the council houses and White House farm. Many years later when the hedge was pulled down Cinny rescued the snake and I still have it. Then we had to pat Peggy the carthorse who would amble across the field to us for a handful of grass. Then we had to swing on the iron railing around the village pond. I'm surprised we got to school at all.

– going to Blakeney Point. It was blazing hot. The mud squelched up between our toes. There was a big hut where we all ate our sandwiches.

– going to the Theatre Royal to see *Peter Pan* with Brenda Bruce. For weeks afterwards us girls being Wendy, strutting round the playground, thrusting out our non-existent bosoms and crying 'You won't forget me will you Peter'.

– garden parties at Miss Robinson's. The garden there smelt like no other. There were lots of bits of wool tied in the bushes which we had to collect. I don't remember why.

– going to North Walsham Secondary Modern to see *The Ice Queen*. There had been heavy snow and we had no transport so Mrs Johnson said 'We'll walk. Walk one step and slide six', and we did. The play was good but I do not know how we got home.

– going on a trip to London and visiting the zoo and the waxworks. We had to travel on the underground at one point and some of the party didn't get on in time. Mrs Johnson said 'Its all right, we're on the circle line we'll just stay on until we come back and get them then.' Like I said, calm.

– nicknames. I can understand why Brian Watts was called Curly and Robin Yaxley Budgie but why on earth was Margaret Wild called Smoker?

– the new council houses being built on the field at the side of the school. One day as we made our way to the field, through the building site, Jill Watts hung some curly wood shavings over her ears and pranced about singing 'And her hair hung down in ringlets'.

– going to Sunday School at the Methodist Chapel. Every year we had an Anniversary where we all had to perform. We all got new clothes for the occasion (which would then be our best dress until next year) and were the bees knees for the day. Auntie Ursula (Fawkes) would play the organ. We had bible quizzes which I tried very hard to win, not because I was particularly devout but the prizes were new books!

– Girls Friendly Society meetings, run by Mrs Cornish, at Trunch Rectory. We put on a play about Derby and Joan in which I had a good speaking part but I woke up on the big day with the measles so there went my glittering stage career.

– the Caravan Mission to Village Children. It was run by Mr and Mrs Moore who had a caravan and a big tent in the meadow which is now the Millennium Field. We would go and pick mushrooms for them for their breakfast. They must have made a big impression on us as when they moved on to Trunch we would cycle over there for the evening service.

– we had a pump in the garden where we got our water. This was shared by several houses and there was also a well a bit further up the road. We had an outside toilet.

– we kept rabbits and Cinny and I would take a sack and fill it with cow weed for them. We also kept chickens and Nan would boil up little potatoes for them and put some sort of red powder in them. It always smelled lovely and I wanted to eat it myself. Our house was never without a dog.

– Mr Payne's ice cream van. Uncle David Lubbock, our next door neighbour was the ice cream man and if we had no money we would quite shamelessly hang about the van until he gave us a cornet. He had a nifty little gadget to make the wafer ice creams like a shallow box on a handle. He put a wafer in the bottom, filled it with ice cream, put another wafer on the top, turned the handle and out popped a perfect wafer ice cream.

– Mr Ward's fish and chip van which came round on a Wednesday night. The chips were lovely and we would rush home to eat them.

– being on the beach and Jill was there with her mum. Jill had a peach, which I had never seen before. She offered me a bite and although I loved the taste I was not too keen on the furry skin.

– the mobile cinema in the village hall. The man who ran it threatened to make Cinny and I leave as we were making too much noise. We weren't being naughty we were just excited.

– shows in the village hall. They would always sing Old Uncle Tom Cobleigh and as the names were sung out a head would pop up from behind a sheet. They were great fun.

– the well yard where we would wind the bucket up to the top and then let go. The bucket would shoot down to the bottom and the handle would whizz round with a very satisfying clank, clank, clank and the wooden well top would shake so much we thought it would fall apart. If we had been hit by that iron handle we wouldn't have lived to tell the tale so we always made sure to jump well clear. (What happened to the well yard by the way?)

– the Green Lane which ran from the back of the station to I don't know where. We had a hide out there and once tried, unsuccessfully I'm glad to say, to cook a mushroom that we found, in a rusty old tin lid.

– the heavy snow of 1947. It was magical. There was a drift at the top of the garden that seemed as big as a house. Uncle Peter made a tunnel through it so Cinny and I could run through.

– taking an old pram out on a Saturday afternoon and filling it with wood for the coming week. The whole family would come and afterwards we always had toasted cheese for tea.

– fruit-picking at Swafield, gooseberries, strawberries and black-currants. One year I earned enough money to buy a new bike from Mr Griffin's shop in North Walsham. It cost £12. Oh the joy of having a brand new bike!

Looking back what strikes me is the amount of freedom that we had. We'd go out in the morning and not get back until teatime with no one knowing where we were. We grew up in a place that always felt safe, and was safe, surrounded by people we knew and who looked out for us. We had a happy time at school and were encouraged in all we did by a wonderful teacher. How lucky we were.

MALCOLM WILD
at Knapton School 1948 to 1955
A retired Police Constable with Norfolk Constabulary.

A chance to remember your early years and putting it down on paper gives other generations their opportunity to share in them.

I was born and brought up in Knapton which is a small part of the triangle formed by the villages of Gimingham, Trimingham, Knapton and Trunch. My mother Margery and Dad William lived in a little flint Cottage at Crossroads, Knapton and I had brother John and sister

Margaret - later two more brothers Keith and Gerald. Mum and Dad had met when he worked on a farm adjoining Knapton House where Mum was in service. The flint cottage was basic with an outside toilet at end of the garden and we would not go out at night without a torch to check nothing ran in under the door! Water was from a well, reached by a bucket and chain and we took it in turns to collect. I would guess that electricity came to our house in about 1945, before this we used oil stoves for cooking and heating water (tin bath in front of fire). Most often we used the smaller room for eating and cooking, the bigger room was for 'best' and only used for special occasions and for visitors.

Neighbours were Harry Sexton an elderly man where I often went and sat in front of his fire and made toast, I also got the taste of cold spuds with salt. On the other side lived Henry and Vera Wild, Henry was a carpenter and an active member of Parish Council up until his death about 2005.

Incidents that I remember at Crossroads includes one evening I was in the rear yard throwing stones when one hit a passing car, the driver quickly stopped and came towards me and I hid in the shed too scared to come out. It was Jack Watts' car, father of Jill Watts, later Shephard. One Sunday morning the area around our house seemed full of galloping horses which had escaped from a field at Hall Lane. With no washing machine or dryer it was very hard work for parents in bringing up a large family and routine was needed with washday on Monday, baking on Friday, cutlery cleaning, ironing, all allocated their own spot. I must have been the youngest pupil at Knapton School taking myself there when I was only three without Mum knowing I had gone. Knapton was a friendly place to live and I could remember most of its residents by name and where they lived - and still can. I went to Sunday School at the parish room with Miss Townsend and Miss Leather. Miss Robinson of Knapton House also helped and she drove a large Lanchester saloon very slowly around the village - I recall its number being UNU 777.

These were my formative years and I often thought living in such a nice village made me a helpful person. Examples included blowing the church organ and later ringing church bells with the Lubbock brothers and Mr Pardon. I also looked after Miss Miles and bringing in her wood and coal. I was paid 2/6 which helped towards to take to the trip from Knapton station to Norwich and go to Carrow Road for the football. On Sundays I sometimes sang in the choir and read a lesson although it meant listening to Revd Thur deliver his boring sermon and wait for the arrival of his wife - always late. I later took my confirmation vows with him. I also attended at the Methodist Chapel to a type of youth club run

118

by Ursula Fawkes and held on two evenings per week. A mixed group of boys and girls attended from Paston and Knapton and each Christmas held a party at Paston Village Hall with jelly, sandwiches and paper hats, etc. Christmas was more fun in those days lasting just a few days and our presents were smaller but we appreciated them much more.

Winters were much more severe with many villages cut off, particularly 1947 when Mundesley was only reachable by walking on tops of the hedges and men of the village combined with sledges to bring in bread and milk for several weeks. The pond at Pond Lane was frequently frozen over with ice thick enough for skating.

Farming was the main work in the villages and Dad worked at Paston Hall Farm and at harvest time took his lunch and cold tea in a bottle inside a sock to keep it warm. He later worked for Mr Guyton at White House Farm, Knapton. When Guyton moved to the farm he brought some of his cattle on the hoof; he was generous and much later gave some land for use as a cycle speedway track. When Dad worked there I often went to the milking shed and 'helped' and to the harvest fields with a small horse and cart collecting straw. I remember how the cut straw cut into my legs. I only had short trousers with short shoes.

I remember playing on the large field in front of the farm with a large 3-wheel push cart with Mr Guyton's niece Beth who was over from Australia. Vaguely I remember on the same field Knapton played football in red and green shirts and on I believe Coronation Day a fête was held which included a cart horse derby which was won by George Wiseman riding bareback on young horse 'Prince'.

Other benefactors in Knapton were Miss Robinson who had a club room with billiard table at Knapton House and when new clubrooms at the rear of Knapton School were built by voluntary labour she gave the table to the club.

Prior to the Beeching cuts Knapton had a railway station with Mr Harrison as station master. The line ran from Mundesley to North Walsham and ran a push and pull steam train which later converted to Diesel units. I was a regular user when I first went to work and the driver would wait for you if you were late and running across the field that runs from Knapton Street

About 1958 the goods yard was well used from September until April loading sugar beet from local farms for transport to Cantley Sugar factory. Often it was a sea of mud and I would go to the cosy workman's hut and sit by an open fire and I made tea and toast and on one occasion oranges that had been washed ashore from a shipwreck were brought on a part-loaded sugar beet trailer to the station. Fruit was scarce after the war and these were very welcome. Social activities in the village included Whit Monday Fête and Barn Dance with live music, at May's Farm and Knapton House held the annual Church Fête – both were always very well attended.

I remember Knapton School for its mixed ages in same class, with the infants painting, and slightly older dancing to music from radio pretending to be trees blowing in the wind. I believe Miss Breeze or Mrs Featherstone was teacher.

In the Big Room we all had desks in which to put our workbooks and Mrs Johnson worked wonders teaching kids of different ages and abilities - our family was a good example with myself, Margaret and John all passing the 11 plus first attempt and then getting our names on a roll of honour in big classroom. Playground football was rather rough on the tarmac but we greatly enjoyed it. Canteen food was brought in from Bacton at about midday and generally very good, amongst my favourites jam pudding with custard. School trips went to Norwich Castle Museum, London Zoo and Blakeney Point where we were escorted around by warden Ted Eales. On one London trip we sat in the stands built for and left standing after the Queen's Coronation. At school I remember Mr Woolgar visiting to show us films and I remember Mr Vic Puncher coming into the school and telling us all that the King had died.

Various tradesmen visited the village, and as I remember them, they were Mr Twigg for milk, bread from Gedges, accumulator for radio from Mr Bridges, groceries from Mr Bryant who called and went through a long list as a memory jogger - the forerunner for today's Home Shopping at the Supermarkets. We also had clothing from Mr Arthurton(?) and sometimes a coloured man with turban called with a suitcase full of ties etc.

Both the School and the Station are now converted to housing. I remember the school's open fires, the tall windows, music and movement on the radio and pretending to be trees blowing in the wind, singing the hymn for those in peril on the sea when the weather was bad, and occasional film shows from Mr Woolgar.

Mrs Johnson was head teacher and was a leading figure in organising the appeal for a playing field in the village - it was sited behind the school and beside the Men's Club also constructed by voluntary helpers and often I would be there 'helping'. Teams played billiards and darts in local leagues.

Cold winters were regular events but the school would remain open. I would cycle to Grammar School using the bus or the train occasionally, I remember Gillian Watts with her large racing type cycle and black cycle bags, cycling to North Walsham High School. All villages had their own tradesmen with Knapton having carpenters (Mr Small, Bob Wright, Bricklayer). Mr Rayner was a painter and they had a blacksmith - his name escapes me. Things I have forgotten to remember and include. Pupils came to Knapton School from Swafield, Trunch, Paston and Edingthorpe. Watching the trees at the large meadow opposite Knapton Hall being felled. Picking primroses on bank near to railway station. Harvesting progressed to combine in about 1960. I still remember learning D.I.Y. by watching Bob Wright and Mr Rayner, and garden double digging from Mr Johnson. Payne's Ice Cream van visited frequently and Mr Ward brought his Fish and Chip van weekly. Shopping was combination of grocery man calling, Paston Post Office (ration book), and walking to local general store. Favourite food – beef steamed pudding and vegetables from Dad's allotment and apple pie and custard.

GORDON HARRISON
at Knapton School 1948 to 1957

My first memories of Knapton School were in 1948 or 1949 (sorry can't remember the exact year but I had already started school at Briston Primary School when I was 5 years old I think.) I left Knapton School at the end of the summer term in 1957.

Living at the station for me was a school boy's dream, my bedroom overlooked the platform and I could watch people boarding and leaving the trains, in the early years some trains would carry on to Cromer and Sheringham, Holt, Fakenham, and up to the Midlands; sometimes their would be 10 carriages. One particular train which came through on a Saturday evening was called the Broadsman; it would be packed with holidaymakers. The later years the trains only went as far as Mundesley and it became known as the push and pull.

The first year or so I was in the infants' class, can't remember who the teacher was in the infants I think Mrs Breeze but I can certainly remember the head teacher Mrs Johnson and also Mrs Featherstone.

The building and playground I can still remember quite well, the big room had five or six rows of double desks with about four desks to the row, Mrs Johnson's desk was at the front to the side of the fireplace which had a big metal fireguard around it, the shelf at the back of the room often had plants of some kind on it. I can remember growing cress on blotting paper; the piano was to her left in the corner, the younger members of the class sat to her left, and we moved down to the other end as we got older. The desks were better down that end with tip up seats.

The little classroom I can't remember very well but I think there must have been about sixteen desks, the infant teachers at the time I attended the school were Mrs Featherstone and Mrs Breeze. I think the meals must have been delivered from another school (?Mundesley or Bacton) to the dinner lady Miss Townsend; they would arrive in stainless steel containers.

The two playgrounds were for boys and girls, as you faced the school the boys were to the left and the girls' playground was to the right, and behind the playground were the school gardens, on the wall of the toilets to the left were painted targets for ball games.

The school gramophone was used for country dancing in the playground, the equipment i.e. (hoops, mats, and balls) also coloured team ribbons I can certainly remember, and there must have been a proper football also cricket stumps and bat. I can remember the time before the playing field which is now Madra. At lunchtime we were allowed to play on the meadow that belonged to Mr Guyton the farmer, that's before and after the council houses were built, the water tower and bungalows came later. We had to try and avoid the cowpats. I can remember several of us catching ringworm from the fence that ran between the meadow and the council houses; in the Coronation year the men of the village played a football match there, they also had an annual cricket match on the field opposite the farm, I don't think the playing field behind the school appeared till 1954/5. Mrs Johnson had a black and white television and would let some of us older boys watch the test match in the summer.

My favourite lessons were PE and Art; also Mrs Johnson used to read a story, usually something from the Famous Five Books on a Friday afternoon. At 13 the boys went to Southrepps School for woodwork lessons this was on a Thursday all day.

In my early years at the school the milk used to be delivered in a small milk churn, can't remember by whom, but later on it was delivered from Twigg's Dairy at Mundesley.

It would take about ten minutes walk to school across the footpath that led from the Station to the village or hitch a lift to school with Freddie Carver the milkman and help him deliver the milk on the way.

School outings I remember were London, the Zoo and the Tower of London, Blakeney Point with a packed lunch, and, depending on the tides when we arrived, we would walk to the point, spend the day among the sand dunes and have a tour of the bird sanctuary and take a boat ride back, or boat out to the point and walk back. Great Yarmouth we went to see the Scottish fishing fleet and watch the fish being landed. The fisher girls then had to gut the fish and pack them in ice. We were allowed to board a small fishing boat called a drifter. I think its name was *The Buckie Thistle* and came from Fraserburgh, the Captain visited the school and gave a short talk about the fishing fleet.

School Holidays were usually taken up by organizing football matches with both Mundesley and Bacton; in the summer time, if not in the harvest field, it would be fruit picking at Mr Banes' fruit farm in Swafield, or potato riddling at Mr Guyton's White House Farm. We had a few chickens and also rabbits, which I looked after.

I can't remember steam threshing in Knapton but I can remember the threshing machine was powered by a big tractor called a Field Marshall and also a horse-operated elevator used for building straw stacks. Some stacks were built in the field belonging to Mr Tom Purdy; they were behind a house at the top of the Station Yard near the entrance to Green Lane, which was a favourite place to play for some of us with plenty of trees to climb.

I did attend Sunday school but decided that I would go where my friends went and that was at the Church Rooms with Ursula Fawkes, and also the Chapel; the preacher was Mr Hicks. Later on I joined the Church Choir and also rang the Church Bells, the parson then was the Reverend Thur who lived at Paston.

I was also a member of the Knapton Men's Club and played for the billiard team and darts team at the age of 14, other members included Henry Wild, John Wild and his father William, Gordon and Eddie Lubbock, Jack Leeder and his son Tony, Jack Stubley, Billy and Stanley Wright, Mervyn Fawkes, John Wright, Bob Wright, Derek & Michael Miller, Stacy Buck, and Chalky White one of my School Masters from North Walsham.

Mrs Dixon ran the Village Shop with another lady, I think her sister? I remember the shop quite well, as we did most of the family shopping there, we had no electricity at the Station so had to rely on paraffin for our lights, and my mother done all cooking on an oil stove and a coal-fired cooking range. I collected the paraffin from the shop, it was also the Post Office, and can remember getting my Grandmother's pension for her.

Mr Dixon kept chickens; he had a large poultry house built opposite the shop and used to supply most people with eggs. He later had more of these poultry houses built at the bottom of the hill near the railway bridge, you would often see him going up and down the hill on a little petrol-driven machine pulling a small trailer.

We never had electricity at the station, but it must have been in the village before we moved there. At the station we used to pump the water from a well near the back door, up into a tank in the roof, but the mains water must have been laid around about 1954/55 because on leaving school in 1956 I worked for W.H. Bullen at Trunch; they were civil engineers, and was involved in connecting the house supplies to surrounding villages.

Village occasions I remember were Church Fêtes at Knapton House - Miss Robinson lived there and she also played the Organ at Church - the Chapel Fête held on the lawn at the front of the house belonging to Mr May in Knapton Street.

I remember children's Christmas parties in the Village Hall, and also the amateur dramatic group at Mundesley would hold concerts in the surrounding villages; one of these actors was Harold Ward a very funny man, who owned Ward's Coaches at Mundesley; he also owned a Fish & Chip van that came round on a Friday evening.

The Coronation in 1953, celebrations were held in a large barn on Mr May's farm in Pond Road. After leaving school in 1957 I worked for W.H. Bullen at Trunch for 9 years, during this time my father had been relocated to Mundesley Station and we moved to the railway house in East View Terrace, Mundesley.

MAUREEN KIRK (STUBLEY)
at Knapton School 1951 to 1958

Until the age of 4 I lived at High House, The Green, Knapton; it had an outside toilet and bath in front of the fire. When we moved to 1 School Close what a marvel it was to have an inside toilet and a bathroom and hot running water. Living next door to the school I used to watch the children at playtime from outside the railings and longed to be with them in school. After a while I was allowed in the playground at playtime. It was so disappointing when they went back into class and I had to go back home with no brothers and sisters to play with. Eventually I was allowed to start school even though I was not quite old enough at the time. How lucky I was to live next door; I used to stay indoors until the whistle went and then ran inside.

During my time at Knapton School I can remember the winters being very cold and the summers being very hot. In the winter how lovely it was to stand in front of the round fire in the Little Room and the open fire in the Big Room, not for long though. In the winter the daily milk used to arrive frozen with the milk rising out of the bottle and the lid like a little cap on the top. It was someone's responsibility to line it up in the hearth so that by break time it had thawed out. On wet days some pupils got wet feet due to leaky shoes and they took their socks and shoes off and put on their gym shoes while their wet things dried over the rails of the fire guard. As each lot became dry another set of socks and shoes or coats were taking their turn. The steam and smell is always to be remembered. One winter, maybe 1956, when we had lots of snow a group of us took our sledges to Stedmans Hill and had great fun tobogganing down the road. We built an igloo house in a snow drift and sat in it most of the afternoon as the blizzards arrived. As it started to get dark we decided it was time to go home and we could not get Keith Wild's legs to bend as he was frozen. We lifted him on to a sledge with knees bent and we pulled him home. Our parents were getting very worried about us all. We were oblivious to all the anxiety and I am glad to say Keith recovered after the ordeal. How wonderful it was to be so free in those days. In summertime it was so warm that the school windows were all open and you could easily be distracted by birds etc. outside. I can remember taking my father's tea to him in the harvest field and also having mine and sitting in the hedgerow eating sandwiches and enjoying the smell of the freshly cut corn. What fun it was to have a ride to the farmyard on top of the corn sacks (never allowed today).

When the doctor came to school for your check-up I can remember how cold it was undressing in the cold porch and standing in your underclothes waiting for your turn. I can remember wearing a liberty bodice to keep warm. I also remember the nit nurse checking through your heads and being relieved when getting the all clear. The biggest dread was the school dentist and everything seemed so painful in those days.

What a treat the school outings were. To live in the country and to go to London was such an experience in those days. I will always remember the huge dinosaur in the Natural History Museum I had never realised just how big it was. The Crown Jewels were so magnificent too. I always found the Royal Tournament so exciting and fun. Going to Blakeney Point was always a special treat especially as I loved birds and the outdoor life. It always seemed a long way to walk across the marshes and the smell of the mud was horrid. It was all worth it when we were able to see the terns nesting and the baby chicks and fascinating how they protected their nests by diving on us as we walked along the path to look at them. After doing lessons in the classroom it was so lovely to go out and see it in real life and see what was in the world, we led such a sheltered life in those days.

We had a special connection to one of the fishing boats that came to Great Yarmouth fishing for herrings. We used to go and visit it once a year. We went down into the mess and had a cup of cocoa, quite horrid. It was a real eye-opener how hard the crew worked and what awful conditions they lived in. The girls who worked on the quayside always worked so hard and it was so cold.

The Church was very important in those days. I used to attend Sunday School in the village hall taken by Miss Townsend and really enjoyed learning about the Bible stories and making things to take home on special dates in the church calendar. I also belonged to the church choir and enjoyed the togetherness on a Sunday. The Church fête was a highlight of the summer and we had great fun bowling for the pig and hoopla etc. We helped with serving the teas after performing country dancing. They were always held at Knapton House the home of Miss Robinson, such a lovely setting.

Knapton School were very happy days, nearly everyone had lived in the village all their lives and everyone knew everyone. Lots of grand-parents lived near and very few people came from further away. There was a real feeling of community spirit in those days. Once the school and the shop closed, that spirit of togetherness disappeared.

RICHARD WILD
at Knapton School 1951 to 1957

Knapton School was a red brick building with a pantile roof and a bell tower. There was one big window in the Little Room and two big windows in the Big Room, a cloakroom with sinks, and a small kitchen. There was a fireplace in each room. There were outside toilets, 4 girls' and 3 boys' plus a urinal painted half way up the wall with bitumen. My grandfather, Mr Joe Bane, used to have the job of emptying them once a week in the garden opposite the school. There were two bicycle sheds, one in each playground. The gardens at the back of the playground were divided into plots which two pupils on each plot looked after. The playground was of asphalt marked out for hopscotch and other games. There were target rings painted on the walls.

We had a piano, radio, gramophone, PE equipment, bats, balls, hoops, mats, skipping ropes, cricket gear. The gramophone was used in the playground for dancing, weather permitting, the piano for hymn singing in the mornings.

Mrs Featherstone was my infant teacher and Mrs Johnson was the teacher in the Big Room. Mrs Spurgeon and Mrs Barrett used to come if one of them was ill. Mrs Watts was the cleaner and Miss Townsend was dinner lady, with Mrs Kirk as helper and playground attendant.

The dinners used to be cooked at Bacton School and brought to Knapton by Mr Pell in metal containers. There was also milk if you wanted it, which used to be heated in winter time.

The school doctor used to come and check us up, also the nurse. We had to go to North Walsham for dental treatment. Mr Rix was the welfare officer who made sure you went to school regularly.

I did not have a favourite lesson, but I liked gardening, nature walks and playing football. I played in the school team with Michael Hicks, Barry Dunham, Patrick Watts, Keith Wild, Peter Woolsey, Peter Featherstone, Roger Buck, Neville Coe, William Schamp and John Lubbock. I failed the scholarship so I went on to North Walsham Secondary Modern School.

At Christmas time we made paper chains trimmings and had a nativity play. Other times in the year we made model Toby jugs, wall plaques and rabbits, and the girls made ballerinas out of plaster of Paris and in rubber moulds. We also did lino-cutting and made raffia mats.

I lived in Pond Cottages in Pond Road in Knapton so it used to take us 15 minutes to walk to school.

I can remember going to London Zoo, Windsor Castle by coach, also going to Blakeney Point to see the seals, also going to Great Yarmouth to see the herring drifters. One in particular was called *Syrious*, from Buckie. We were allowed to go on board to see where the herring were stored and where the crew slept.

I attended Methodist Sunday School in Pond Road 10 a.m. to 10.45 a.m. Our teachers were Ursula Fawkes, Jessie Rose, Herbert Hicks, and Iris Carr. I also went to Christian Endeavour on Tuesday evenings.

We did the shopping at Dixon's in the Street, and International Stores in North Walsham who delivered the groceries to the door, as did Mr F Bird, the butcher, and Burtons with the bread and Mr Twigg with the milk. Mr Jack Larke delivered the coal and wood.

The water we got out of a well in the garden opposite our house. We had a bucket toilet at the top of the garden. Mother cooked in a wall oven and kitchen range, and on an oil stove. We also had a copper, and all this was in the kitchen.

I think having a goose for Christmas dinner was a real treat.

We had a garden and an allotment. We kept pigs, chickens, rabbits, cockerels, and ducks on the pond. We also had a dog, cat and goldfish.

I had to muck out the pigs and rabbits, and feed them, and collect grass and hogweed for the rabbits, and also take the dog for walks and help in the garden and allotment.

I can remember Whit Monday fêtes at Church Farm, followed by a barn dance. I won first prize in the fancy dress as a waiter. Dad won bowling for the pig, that is how we came to keep them. We also used to trim up our bicycles for a competition. There were also fêtes at Knapton House by kind permission of Miss Robinson. There were socials and concerts in the Parish Room. On Shrove Tuesday there was a pancake social where ladies cooked pancakes on oil stoves. I had too many one year, which put me off them.

There were the Happisburgh Players that came and did a concert. Also Knapton had the Black and White Minstrels who were myself, Mum and Dad, my sister Jennifer, my uncle William Wild with his sons John and Keith, my aunt Margery Schamp, and Mary Puncher. Mrs Carr took us for singing lessons and played the piano.

The first combine harvester I can remember was a tractor-drawn Claas. It was owned by Mr Basey Fisher at Strathearn Farm. I can also remember steam thrashing at Mr Claydon's at Parr's Farm in Hall Lane. I can remember a steam roller which rolled stones in on the tarred roads. It was owned by Plumbly and Gaze at North Walsham.

CRYSTAL THOMPSON (PYE)
at Knapton School 1951 to 1958

Going down the 'Memory joggers' list these are my memories:

1. Desks with the lift up lid, the inkwells at the corner and dip pens, which I found did not make writing very easy.

2. I remember a male supply teacher helping out, who made us do a 'hexagon' which I could not work out and got upset, but I always remembered how many sides it had by this.

3. I was with Mrs Johnson although I must have been with someone else first, but my memories were in the big room. We often talk with our children of our school days, when the 'nit nurse' came and we would line up to get our hands/nails checked and she would look through our hair. (Perhaps this would solve the problem today with the nits).

4. I still have a 'Singing Together' book, which again my children find strange that this was taught with the radio. Making things with papier maché comes to mind, also sewing/embroidery making mats, which were a large version of today's cross stitch which my mum had, and following her death has come back to me.

5. Another of the memories was the 'pinks' in the garden, and picking them, which I guess were sold for school funds.

6. Small bottles of milk, which I think were ⅓ of a pint, in winter were sitting in the fireplace to thaw as they were frozen when delivered, with ice above the top and the lid sitting on top of the ice.

7. As I lived in the village I walked to school, but when I left and went to North Walsham Secondary Modern School, I cycled whatever the weather. The choice was to go by train, be supplied with a school bike or use your own bike (which I did) and was paid 6 shillings and 8 pence a term (1 pound per year - old money) to maintain it.

8. The outings to Blakeney Point to see the terns nesting and with the young chicks were happily remembered also going to Gt Yarmouth to see and go on the Scottish fishing boat when it came down for the herring season.

9. I went to the Sunday School in the church rooms, I think that was ran by Miss Robinson and Miss Townsend, and getting a stamp at the end of each Sunday to take home and stick in a book.

10. We lived down the street at Knapton until I was 9 years old and a bath was taken in the living room and in front of an open fire in the wintertime. I remember an oval tin bath, which would have been used for myself, and a large oblong one that was used by my parents. The toilet was at the bottom of the garden. The water was cranked up from the well, which served about 5 houses.

11. The shopping was done from the local village shop which was owned by my mum's aunt and uncle and she helped in the shop for some years until they retired.

12. Dad had 2 allotments: one was near the school where he had pigs, chickens and grew vegetables and the other was between Mundesley Road and Pond Road which was larger and he had sugar beet one year and corn the alternate one. I helped with the sugar beet, digging them from the ground with a small two-pronged fork. It was lovely when

the day-old chicks came and we collected them from the train at Knapton station in their boxes. We had a golden Labrador named Flossy, which was bought as a puppy as I was frightened of dogs.

13. The yearly fêtes at Knapton House the home of Miss Robinson, were something to look forward to, with the lovely large garden, and I was also in the Brownies which was run by Mrs Macmillan and held at her house in Hall Lane which also had lovely gardens to play in.

DAVID WHITE
at Knapton School 1954 to 1960

We moved into Knapton on 10th October 1954, my Mum's birthday, when I was 5 years old. I had started my education at Elsing (another primary school now closed) in the same year. We lived in Lyng then, but I was born in Trimingham, at home, on 7th February 1949.

We lived in Hall Lane until about 1962, when Dad worked as pigman for Mr Cargill, and at 2 The Green later. On our arrival at Hall Lane, there was cold running water in the form of one tap in the kitchen. This was an improvement on the well shared by four homes at Lyng, but the lavatory at Hall Lane was a bucket affair in a detached outhouse, emptied once a week after dark by the 'night soil' men. No modernisation was carried during our time there.

It was no better at the Green when we moved there in 1962, Dad having left farm work and started in the building trade, working for Chris Cork's father in North Walsham, but modernisation was carried out courtesy of Norfolk County Council about two years later. This consisted of inside bathroom and toilet downstairs and hot water via an immersion heater and back-boiler. Heating, however, continued to be by open coal fire.

The School
I used to walk to school with my sister and brother and the Puncher family, who lived nearby.

I think the Big Room and Little Room at Knapton were so named, not because one was bigger than the other - although that may have been the case - but rather in reference to the relative size of the youngsters who occupied them from 9 a.m. to 3.30 p.m. Monday to Friday.

Mrs Johnson (Head) and Mrs Featherstone were the teachers during all of my time there; excellent teachers, maintaining good order and giving us a sound start in life. I still remember lots that we learned there.

130

The lessons all seemed to merge into one another in a way, but the subjects included English, sums (maths), history, geography, scripture, music ('Singing Together') nature study, craft, dancing and gardening.

I don't remember much about Mrs Breeze, who I think was a supply teacher that filled in when required, but I do remember Mr Mundy (not sure about the spelling), a very strict and scary man, who used to draw maps of Britain freehand from memory on the blackboard, which really impressed me, and taught us how to draw hexagons with compasses in a honeycomb pattern, boring us all to tears!

'Singing Together' was on the wireless (radio) once a week. We had the books and the man on the wireless used to teach them to us and we would sing along. Later in the week, Mrs Featherstone would play them on the piano in the Big Room for us all to sing to. If Mrs Johnson had to play, she would play with just one finger.

PE (I think we used to call it PT, for Physical Training) was gymnastics of sorts in the playground. We wore coloured bands over one shoulder. (What were they for?)

At playtime, we would play games passed down from goodness-knows-when; games like 'What's the Time, Mr Wolf?', a game we called 'staggy' (a kind of tag), skipping with ropes, jacks, etc. In the lunch break, the boys would play football, or sometimes cricket in the summer, on the playing field (which must have been laid down in about 1958, because I can remember it being done).

Fridays was when the pre-school children joined us. We played games on the field in the afternoon. Mrs Johnson's favourite was rounders for everyone.

Not many of us liked dancing lessons, a mixture of ballroom and barn dancing, usually done with the aid of the gramophone in the playground next to the school house. Dances I remember the names of are The Gay Gordons and The Circassian Circle.

I remember the library van that used to arrive once in a while at the school gates at 3.30, so that the mums could borrow books as well as the children. My favourite visitor, however, was Mr Woolgar, who used to bring his 16mm projector and show us films such as 'Muffin the Mule', 'Mr Pastry' and educational films on special days such as Christmas and the end of term.

Life in the village

There were very few motor vehicles in those days and even fewer television sets. Just one channel (BBC) in those days, with ITV following, then BBC2 in about 1960.

Knapton School on the playing field with Mrs Johnson and Mrs Featherstone c. 1957

People with cars that I can remember were: Mr Hicks, (Sunbeam Rapier SAH 888), Mr Burlingham, the foreman at Mr Cargill's farm (--- 282), Mr Macmillan (cousin of the then prime Minister, it was said) who lived at the Old Hall, Miss Robinson of Knapton House (a Lanchester, 777 UNU) and Mr Guyton (a car with a personalised plate JLG ---).

This was the time of horses being replaced by tractors but I can remember Mr Cargill's cart horses, Billy, a brown horse, and Prince, who was white.

My dad, Victor, was a keen gardener, probably out of necessity, and worked hard to keep all five of us virtually self-sufficient in fresh vegetables most of the year round. At Hall Lane, he had three large vegetable plots and a large plot at the back of 2 The Green. Livestock at home included at various times chickens, Muscovy ducks and rabbits. The problem with the rabbits was that we children used to give them names and treat them as pets. But Dad had other ideas and either Powder - or was it Puff? - ended up on our dinner plates one night. Rest assured Dad was made to feel very guilty!

At first, when we had no car, shopping was done at the local post office store in The Street, where 'Cornerstones' is now. In addition, groceries were ordered from and delivered by Rust's and meat from J. O. Kent, both of North Walsham. Bread was delivered by Mr Drury and milk from someone else. Later, when Dad acquired his very first car, a sit-up-and-beg Ford Anglia (807 PNG, I think), he and Mum would drive into North Walsham for the weekly shop.

The annual village fête at Church Farm was an event not to be missed. Side shows and stalls included the White Elephant Stall, Cake Stall, Bowling for the Pig, Quoits, etc. Takings usually exceeded £100, which in those days constituted a roaring success.

Church and Sunday School
From moving into the village, we started attending the Methodist Chapel at the kind invitation of Mr Herbert Hicks, local preacher and the Sunday School Superintendent. I, with my sister Sylvia and brother Philip, attended the Sunday School, which started at 10.15 and Mum and Dad went with us to the evening services at 6.30. Later I joined the junior choir, run by Mrs A. Carr of Verbena Cottage on the Street and started going to the 11 o'clock service where the choir led the hymn singing. I later became a teacher in the Sunday School and one of the organists. Mrs Carr was my music teacher and she used to make a small charge (2s. 6d. or 5s. which she donated to the Spastics Society.)

On 2 nd December 1967, it was my privilege to play the organ for my sister Sylvia's wedding to Tony Minns of Happisburgh.

The annual Sunday School trip was to Great Yarmouth, funded largely by the proceeds from the fête. A coach was hired, usually from Starlings in North Walsham, and pocket money was given out on the way and was spent mostly on the fun-fair. There was no youth group at Knapton during my time there, but we went instead to Trunch, where young people from neighbouring villages met once a month at Brick Kiln Farm, the home of Mr Wally Hicks. A good time of fellowship was had by all, with singing and visiting speakers.

It is a pleasure for me and my wife, Joan, when visiting my family in Norfolk, to pop into the Chapel on a Sunday morning and enjoy worship and a cup of tea with old friends, who always give us a very warm welcome.

Moving on

I finished at Knapton County Primary in 1960 and, having failed the 11 Plus at the final stage, started at North Walsham Secondary Modern. From there, I went on to do O and A level GCEs at Great Yarmouth College of Further Education before starting work in 1968 at the Norwich Union in Surrey Street, whom I have served faithfully in Norwich, Leeds and Manchester for some 37 years, breaking for just one year to attend a course at Cliff College, where I met Joan. But that's another story! Now I am looking forward to retirement, which should give me more time to revisit the homeland and catch up once again with old friends.

JUNE WILD (WILD)
at Knapton School 1956 to 1962

Before starting school properly in 1956, I went on a Friday afternoon. For all my time in the Little Room, I had Mrs Featherstone as my teacher. She has since told me she always knew when it was near school finishing time at 3.30 p.m. as from her desk facing the window she could see my mother go to feed the chickens on our garden opposite the school.

Years earlier, my grandfather John Wild emptied the school's outside toilets (which were still there when I went to school) on to that garden. When he died in 1932, either my grandmother or Miss Robinson who then owned the garden, let Joe Bane have a piece of the garden to crop as

Knapton Christian Endeavour and Youth Fellowship 1952

Sitting on the floor, left to right: Cecil Yaxley, Brian Wild, Christopher
  Hicks
Left of Christmas Tree, front row, left to right: Jenny Wild Cynthia
  Croxon, Ruth Steward, Ann Lubbock, Joan Puncher, Muriel Gee
  Second row, left to right: Barbara Puncher, Jackie Croxon, Janet
  Steward, Jill Watts
  Third row, left to right: Jessie Rose, Yvonne Lee, Margaret Wild,
  Anne Lee, Shirley Wright
Right of Christmas Tree, front row, left to right: Unknown, Malcolm
  Wild, Unknown
  Second row, left to right: Betty Wright, Robin Yaxley, John Wright,
  Michael Miller
  Standing at the back, left to right: John Wild, David Hicks, Ursula
  Fawkes, Brian Puncher

he had taken over the job of emptying the toilets on to the garden.

When I went into the Big Room my teachers were Mrs Johnson, then for short spells Mrs Spurgeon, Mrs Grigg, before Mrs Addison became the new head teacher and lived in the school house.

I can remember reciting the times tables and learning to read. We could take books home to read. In 1960 I got first prize for a year's work for writing. It was called 'My Book' and was done like a diary. The prize was a book of British Birds, signed by Mrs Johnson. I still have it. We also took part in essay competitions for schools organised by Cadbury Brothers Ltd, where we gained certificates of merit. Also there was an art competition to do with Brooke Bond.

We had lessons from the radio, one being 'Singing Together'. We went to the Church Rooms (now Arden Kitchens) in North Walsham for singing festivals, and had a packed lunch at the High School. On fine days we had the gramophone outside for country dancing, which we did once at a fête at Miss Robinson's of Knapton House, and also at the Secondary Modern School at North Walsham. There we also saw *A Midsummer Night's Dream* with Mrs Grigg.

During the mornings, we had a third of a pint bottle of milk to drink. As I lived at the crossroads, I went home for dinner. It was only a two minute walk. Miss Townsend was the dinner lady. The dinners came by car from Bacton. My mother (Vera Wild) during the war worked for a while at the school when the kitchen was built on to the school.

At dinner time, Mrs Kirk was in the playground and was also the cleaner at the school. Mrs Kirk could also be found with us, holding the end of a very big skipping rope which we jumped into. A lot of the time we played on the playing field by the swings, and sometimes did not hear the whistle go and were late back into the classroom.

We went into the school house to watch on the television a royal wedding. It may have been Princess Margaret's, then another time into Mrs Kirk's house who lived next door to the school, to watch another royal wedding.

School holidays consisted of about 2 weeks at Christmas, 3 weeks at Easter and 5 to 6 weeks in the summer, with half terms of a few days, and with days off for the Royal Norfolk Show.

I can remember Mr Rix the school welfare officer coming to the school, and Mr Woolgar coming to show films at the Christmas Party. We made chains for Christmas decorations out of thin strips of coloured paper with the ends stuck together, and wings for the angels made of cardboard with tissue paper stuck on to it, or cotton wool, for the nativity plays which took place in the Parish Room.

After school for school funds we would sell bunches of pinks that were grown in the school garden, and whist drive tickets. We each had our own part of the village to do.

We had school outings to London, we left Knapton early by train, and went on the tube, once in London. We visited the Tower of London, the Zoo, Trafalgar Square, one of the museums, a boat trip on the Thames, and went into one of the big shops.

Each summer we had a day out on Blakeney Point, went by coach, then by boat across to the Point. After lunch we walked back in the mud to the coach. I left the school in July 1962 to go to the Secondary Modern School in North Walsham.

Knapton Church Sunday School

I attended the Church Sunday School, and we younger ones had our lessons in the church, taught by Miss Leather, which lasted about 30 minutes. We only filled one of the pews a little way down on the left side of the church.

Some Sundays we had a lift home by Miss Robinson in her car. We had two parties a year at Knapton House. The summer one was outside and when leaving, Miss Robinson gave each of us a big bunch of dahlias to take home. The winter party was held indoors with tea in the library served by Agnes Gee, followed by games, one being Hunt the Thimble in the dining room.

When we were older we went to the Sunday School in the Parish Room taken by Miss Townsend; there was a small table with a cross on it, in front of the stage, the rows of chairs facing it, but we younger ones had our lessons in the small room to the right of the stage (now the kitchen) with Mrs Plant. When it was time for us to join the older ones, the numbers had gone down, and I think Miss Townsend had finished teaching, so Mrs Plant taught the few of us left round a table.

Once a year during the summer, we went to the eleven o'clock service in the church, taken by the Reverend Thur, where we stood in a line in front of the congregation and read from the Bible. We had an outing once a year to Great Yarmouth with Revd and Mrs Thur, and joined by Paston children and parents.

Knapton Men's Club

My mother was cleaner of the Men's Club, and when I came out of school winter months (it was closed summer time) we would go and she would clean up from the previous night. It was heated by an open fire in the billiard room which you entered into from the front porch.

There was also a darts room and a small kitchen, in which on home match nights on a Thursday, the cups and saucers were laid out. (My job!) The tea was made in a big urn at home when about 8.30 p.m. Dad and another member would come and carry the urn back to the clubroom. Mum also made the cheese rolls.

Once I was allowed to go and help with the refreshments as Miss Robinson was presenting the prizes. During the summer school holiday, my mother spring-cleaned the Club. I helped with washing the paint-work, but I liked it better playing darts in the darts room.

Knapton Village

I lived next door to the then Parish Room and the cottage always held a key to the Room, as it did in my grandparents' time (John and Mary Ann Wild), which was home to my father Henry and his sisters, Gladys, Lily and Olive.

My grandmother helped at functions held in the Room, one being making tea and supper for 20 bell-ringers, with Dad carrying the water from the well yard at the end of the little road. I can remember the well being filled in.

Dad took over the cottage from his late parents and my mother was the cleaner of the Parish Room for several years, and also helped at functions. I can remember social evenings on a Shrove Tuesday, with the pancakes being cooked on oil stoves on the stage.

Mum would help at wedding receptions and I would go in with her. The kitchen was just inside the door, where the toilets are now, and I would peer round. I can picture now a bride dancing wearing a lovely white dress.

Ladies and children could be seen on a Saturday afternoon looking over the church wall to see the weddings. I was 10 when I was a bridesmaid there for my cousin Betty Wright's wedding.

Fêtes were held each year at Miss Robinson's, for the church, and another for the W.I. and Men's Club who shared the proceeds. Dad would be on Bowling for the Pig. I would help and one year the gentleman who opened the fête paid for me to have a go. I won! But did not have the pig, but £5 instead.

I can remember electricity always being in the home, but for a while we cooked on an oil stove which had rings on the top for saucepans and the oven was big enough for a chicken.

Our garden, where Dad grew vegetables and kept chickens and I had a rabbit for a while (I also had a cat at home), was opposite the school and it went with the cottage. In my grandmother's time that is where she had to go to hang her washing. It was called the drying ground.

The cottage had a small garden at the front, and Mum shared the linen line at the back with Mrs Pooley who lived next door. We had no back door then so Mum had to walk round to the little road with her washing. The garden at the back was open all around Miss Adams' wooden bungalow, plenty of flower beds and some grass where she would let me play.

We did our shopping at Dixon's shop in the village. It was also the Post Office. We got our meat from Mundesley and the Co-op butcher in North Walsham. From Mundesley twice a week we had groceries delivered and bread three times a week. Milk was delivered daily, as were newspapers from the shop at Knapton, and then by Brian Wild.

My jobs at home were helping inside the home, and getting rabbit food from down the Hall Lane. I cannot remember any one meal as a special treat, but what I do remember is what I did not like, and that was pig's fry!

PEARL HICKS (EVES)
at Knapton School 1956 to 1962

Herbert Hicks (Pearl's father) was school governor for several years. He attended school plays and sports days, giving out prizes. He was Sunday School superintendent of the Knapton Methodist Church for over 40 years. Sunday mornings he would go to Paston and collect 6 to 8 children in his car to bring to Sunday School (wouldn't be allowed now!) An annual highlight was the Sunday School Anniversary. People walked from Trunch and Paston for an afternoon and evening service. We would entertain lots of people for tea. Mrs Carr from Verbena Cottage ran a small choir for a few years. She was very strict but a good teacher. She also taught music from her home.

The Methodist Church held an annual fête at the Church Farm. People prepared for this months in advance. A memory is of ladies waiting at the jumble stall waiting for the prices to drop.

My mother, Margaret Hicks (Turner), now 93, attended Knapton School. Miss Janet Carpenter was then head mistress. Mum would go to the school house after school, and she knitted all Miss Carpenter's wool suits.

Monday mornings at school was banking day when I was there. I took my two shillings and sixpence in every week. Mr Pell from Bacton was the dinner man. Miss Townsend served school dinners, always spoiling me with extra beetroot, my favourite.

ANDREW CLAYDON
at Knapton School 1957 to 1963

Andrew started school in 1957. Teachers were Mrs Featherstone in the little room and Mrs Johnson in the big room. Mrs Grigg came to teach for a little while.

The little room had a tortoise stove in one corner with a fireguard railing round it. In winter the milk bottles were put there, which were drunk at playtime in the morning. One day, Mrs Featherstone put little bits of wax crayon in the stove. The classroom then had to be evacuated because the chimney nearly caught fire. The school had outside toilets which were draughty in the winter!

Andrew can remember Mr Rix, the attendance man, coming into the school, Mrs Kirk in the playground at dinner time, Miss Townsend as the dinner lady. He biked to school but at dinnertime, which was from 12 to 1.15 p.m. he went to Granny Claydon at Parr's Farm for a cooked lunch. He could also be found there after school. He said he could bike very quickly and be gone. Then his mother would have to wait for him when she came to pick him up as Granny would say 'He's gone again'. He could then be found helping to feed the pigs on his grandfather's farm, and helping out at harvest time.

School trips were to Blakeney Point and to London by train to visit the Zoo and the Science Museum. Sports Days were held on the playing field. Nativity plays took place in the Parish Room with Andrew playing one of the Wise Men. Christmas parties were at the school when Mr Woolgar came in to show films in the big room. Also at Christmas time, making coloured chain decorations.

After the 11 plus, Andrew left Knapton School in 1963 to go to the Secondary Modern School at North Walsham.

Andrew went to the Church Sunday School with Miss Leather as teacher, where she would put a picture sticker in your album for attendance. Christmas parties were held at Miss Robinson's at Knapton House. She drove a Lanchester car. The older children had Sunday School in the Parish Room. On a Sunday in the summer, the children were lined up in church to read from the Bible. Andrew said he used to read his piece very quickly with head down, not looking up at all! He also rang the church bells for a while when he was 12.

Fêtes were held at Miss Robinson's at Knapton House. The village shop was down the street, owned by Mr 'Tarts' Dixon. The family also shopped in North Walsham. Father would shoot a lot of rabbits, so to have roast beef and Yorkshire pudding was a lovely treat. Andrew can

**Knapton Methodist Sunday School with the
Scripture Union Shield around 1954**

On the ground, left to right: Michael Bowles, Mary Puncher, Pearl
Hicks, Mary Steward, Edna Puncher
Sitting, left to right: Ruth Steward, Patricia Wild, Rodney Rose, Cynthia
Croxon, Muriel Gee, Richard Wild, Joan Puncher
Standing, left to right: Bruce Rudd, Barbara Puncher, Rodney Edwrads,
Mr Hicks, Janet Steward, Jenny Wild, Roy Fawkes, Jackie Croxon,
Brian Wild, Ursula Fawkes, Jessie Rose, Iris Carr, Eric Steward,
David Hicks, Chris Hicks

remember thrashing with a tractor at Cargill's, Puncher's, Dan Dixon's, and his grandfather's, whose first combine was a Massey Harris 726. The family always had a garden, and kept pigs, goats, chickens, bullocks and cows. He can remember a crater in the third field on the left down the Mundesley Road, where a bomb had dropped during the war.

After attending Easton Agricultural College, Andrew went as tractor driver on Cargill's farm, in 1979 became foreman, and in 1985 farm manager. In 1993 he took on the tenancy of the Clan Trust Farm at Edingthorpe.

Nativity Play in the Parish Room 1953
'The Studded Door'

Part 4

Accounts by some people on specific topics

PAMELA DIXON (GARNHAM)

The Shop

When we first moved to Knapton Mrs Smith had the shop and Post Office in her front sitting room at the bottom of the Street. In 1948-9 she sold the business due to ill health. My father bought it.

Outside the Shop, 1948
Miss Townsend, Mrs Dixon, Pamela Dixon, Babs Dixon and Dolly,
and Louise

Everything was still on ration books and in short supply. Someone came from Norwich Head Post Office for several days to teach us how to do the accounts etc. Ration Book customers had to register with a shop. It was very difficult when we were allocated a few tins of fruit or salmon. We tried to be fair to our registered customers. Biscuits came in big square tins. We could also get tins of broken ones which were much cheaper.

When clothes came off coupons, I can remember large boxes of wellie boots, caps, braces, men's trousers, socks, ladies' underwear,

143

nighties, aprons, jumpers and lisle stockings, and nylons (if we could get them). Everything sold very quickly as clothing was scarce during the war.

When sweets came off ration they were still very short and we could never seem to get enough to meet demand.

We used to go to Fayers bakehouse every Friday, and bring back trays of cakes to sell. Later we had a weekly delivery of Melton Mowbray pies which were very popular, mince, steak and kidney, and chicken, as well as pork.

The Post Office accounts had to be added up and tally every week, and pension dockets etc. sent to Norwich. That had to be done every night. Pay wasn't very good. When I finished in 1981, the wage was just over £30 per week.

Later we did the newspaper round. Barbara and I used to cycle before work. On a Saturday we would load up the van with orders to deliver also a selection of groceries and a lot of Corona, very popular at that time. Dad and I used to go round the village collecting newspaper money and delivering groceries and selling from the van.

In later years, as supermarkets started to open and more people got cars, the trade slowly dropped until at the end my cousin Violet Thompson and I just kept it going until we could sell up after my mother died. (Mrs Dixon lived in the house which adjoined the shop)

WILLIE PUNCHER

Changes in Farming

Over the last 60 years, farming has changed beyond belief.

When horses were used, one man and two horses and a single furrow plough used to do one acre per day. Now one man and a large tractor pulling a 5 to 6 furrow plough can do 15 or 20 acres per day.

After ploughing, the ground was rolled and harrowed, then drilled with horses. Now the tractor pulls a cultivator with drill attached, everything done with one pass.

With the help of plant breeders, sprays for pests and disease, yields have gone up from one and a half to two tons an acre to four tons an acre, in wheat.

The early combines had a six to eight foot cutter bar, and did one to one and a half acres per hour. Now some of the large machines have a cutter bar of 30 foot and can do 60 to 70 acres a day.

The sugar beet crop has seen major changes. In the past, after the crop came up, horses were used to pull a horse hoe to kill the weeds between the rows. Men spent hours of back-breaking work hoeing each row and leaving one plant every eight or nine inches. Now the crop is set by a drill which leaves one seed every 7, 8 or 9 inches. For weed control they are sprayed 3 times, once as soon as the crop is set, and twice after the crop is emerging. So no hand-work at all. Here again, with the help of plant breeders and sprays, yields have more than doubled in the past 60 years. Up to the early 50s, the crop was dug and topped by hand. Each man looked to do one acre per week. Some did a little more. That was real hard work, out in the middle of a field in November and December, with rain, cold and gales. Some of the tractor drivers of today in their heated cabs would not last 5 minutes doing the same job.

From the early 50s, machines started to appear to lift the crop, one row at a time, pulled by a tractor delivering the beet into tractor and trailer running alongside. Over the years, machines got larger, doing 2, 3 and 4 rows at a time. Now they are large self-propelled machines doing 6, 9 and 12 rows at a time, 20 to 30 acres a day. A lot different from one man one acre per week.

The potato crop has also seen huge changes in production of the crop. Years ago, the potatoes were set by hand, men carrying trays or baskets, dropping a potato every 10 to 12 inches into pre-opened furrows, which were then ridged up. Weed control was by cultivation between the rows. Now the ground is ridged up and stone picked, and the potatoes set by a tractor pulling a 2 to 4 row planter, and ridged up all in one operation. Weed control is by one spray just as the potatoes are coming up. Yields have gone up from 8 to 10 tons per acre years ago, to 18 to 25 tons per acre today. This again is due to plant breeders and sprays, mostly for blight control. Lifting the crop has also changed from years ago when the potatoes were spun out of the ground, and gangs of men and women' picked them up. More back-breaking work. Now tractors pulling 2 row harvesters can lift 6 to 8 acres per day. Years ago the crop was stored outside in the field where it had been lifted, by making a long clamp, covering it with straw and then earth to protect from frost. Today, most of the crop is stored in temperature-controlled buildings.

To sum it all up, over the past 60 to 70 years farming has changed from very labour-intensive and hard work, to today's farm worker sitting in his heated air conditioned cab with the radio on.

In the last war, farmers had to plough up every last acre for food. Now we get paid to leave land idle when there are millions starving in the world, and when the bio-fuels industry is starting to take off. There should not be one acre left idle. I think in 20 to 30 years' time, farming will turn full circle and every acre will be cropped again. I hope so.

JUNE WILD (WILD)

Knapton Men's Club
a history compiled from the minutes of the Club since 1938

On 2 November 1938, a General Meeting was held in the Parish Room to form a Men's Night Club; about 30 men were present. The following names are today still remembered by many in Knapton, and descendants are still living there.

The Rev. Prichard was elected chairman, with Mr T. A. Claydon as Treasurer, and Mr Elijah Coe as Secretary. The Committee was Mr R. Kirk (who was also caretaker), Mr G. Gaze, Mr W. Small, Mr R. Wright, Mr H. Wild, Mr F. Pardon, and Mr H. Fawkes. Mr N. May was opted on to the Committee in January 1939.

There were donations of a darts board from Dr Gutch, from Miss Robinson a bagatelle board, from Mr May 5 packs of playing cards and a table tennis table.

The Parish Room was to open on a Monday, Wednesday and Friday, from 6.30 p.m. to 10 p.m. Entrance was 3d and boys under sixteen 2d. The caretaker was to be paid 8/- a month. It was also decided that men working in the village and friends of members would be able to come on payment of 3d per week.

The first list of members totalled 48 on 25 January 1939. A Whist Drive and Dance was held to raise money for the 'Rebuilding Fund' of a new club. Burton's Band was asked to play the music. Entrance was fixed at 1/3 for whist, dance and refreshments, and for the dance only 9d. Mr Small was doorkeeper, and Mr Coe the MC for the whist drive. Mr Claydon was asked to arrange the refreshments. It must have been successful as another was fixed for 12 April 1939.

The Club closed for the summer months ending with a supper on 28 April 1939 for members, consisting of a 14 lb joint of salt beef, 10 lb joint of roast beef, pickles, bread rolls, cheese and biscuits, a bottle of ale for each man and cigarettes and tobacco. Entertainment was provided by

Mr Sparkman from Spa Commons and Mr G. Kirk sang songs during the evening.

War was declared on 3 September 1939. The club however, continued. The General Meeting was held on November 16 1939. The following were elected:- Chairman Mr Prichard, Vice Chairman Mr N. May, Secretary Mr Fawkes. There was a vote of thanks to Mr Coe (who was station master in the village) for his services and regret expressed that the blackout conditions should cause his resignation (because he had responsibility for this very important task during the war). The Committee was Mr H. Wild, Mr R. Wright, Mr Gaze, Mr Steward, Mr Small, Mr F. Pardon, and Mr G. Turner. Blackout arrangements had to be made, and Mr May provided frames for the windows. The Club provided the material to screen the frames for blackout, which Mr Claydon supervised.

Money-raising whist drives continued, with proceeds for the Club. The proceeds of the whist drive on 15 December 1939 were divided between the Club and the Comforts Fund of the Mundesley and District British Legion.

In April 1940, the Club sent a money order of 4/6 to each of the 13 men of the parish serving in the forces, and 18/- was handed to the Knapton Working Party for the Troops. The last minutes during the war were dated September 1941, but we can assume that subscriptions, opening hours and seasons remained the same until the next recorded minutes, on October 18 1946.

These minutes record the election of officers and committee. The Rev. Prichard and Mr Norman May remained as chairman and vice chairman, and Mr Henry Wild became the secretary. The winter season started on 21 October, and subscriptions were raised to 6d per week for members and 3d for boys between 14 and 16. A donation was given to the Trustees of the Parish room for its use.

At the General Meeting on 16 December 1946, Mr May said that he and other members had visited Miss Robinson to see if members might have the use of her billiard room at Knapton House. (We are not told if this is because the Parish Room was more in demand after the war by other groups, or indeed if there had been some kind of dispute.) In any case, Miss Robinson agreed to the use of her room, but £9 5s had to be found to install electric light, and to provide the money, a whist drive was held on 3 January 1947. The committee dealt with the preparations of the room, and it was opened on Tuesday and Thursday nights. New committee members, Ronnie Coe, Eddie Lubbock and Eric Wright were elected, and it was agreed that a member of the committee should be responsible for the room each time it was used.

A General Meeting was held on 15 September 1947. Arthur Claydon and Kenneth Lee joined the Committee. The secretary was given permission to purchase any games needed, and an oil stove to heat the billiard room. Arrangements were made to have the room cleaned once a week.

At a Committee meeting on 19 September 1947, Mr William Wild stated that League games would be played on Thursday nights, starting at 7 p.m. So far, 10 teams had been entered. Members playing League games away paid 2/- per head for transport, the Club paying the rest. A Starlings bus from North Walsham provided the transport.

At the General Meeting on 4 March 1949, it was reported that Miss Robinson had told the Club secretary that if the Men's Club chose to build a place of their own, she would present them with her billiard table. This offer was gratefully accepted. More fund-raising events were arranged, a garden fête to take place at Knapton House, by kind permission of Miss Robinson, and a Barn Dance to take place at Church Farm, by kind permission of Mr May.

At the Committee meeting on 16 March 1949, the chairman Rev. Prichard and the secretary reported on a meeting they had had with Mr Cargill to see if the Club could purchase a piece of land on which to build the new Club. At a later date, Mr Cargill replied that the Club could have a piece of land on a 99 year lease. A proposed plan of the new building was then shown to Mr Cargill for his approval.

At a General Meeting on 25 March 1949, three Trustees, Mr May, Mr Henry Wild and Mr William Wild were appointed for the new proposed building. A Committee meeting was held on 8 April 1949, to discuss arrangements for the money-raising fête to be held on 16 July. More members were co-opted on to the Committee to help with the fête. Mr May offered to approach his brother, Mr Arthur May, to see if the meadow opposite Knapton House could be used, and to see Miss Purdy for the hoop-la, and Major Bardolph Wilkinson for the treasure hunt. Mr W. Wild offered to manage the darts, and Mr George Wild the bowling for the pig. The Rev. Prichard gave a donation to assist the Club to buy a pig and saw Mr Bridges about music and ices. Miss Robinson, Miss Leather, and Mrs May were asked to do catering for the day, and Mrs Johnson (headmistress) if the school children could provide entertainment.

A General Meeting was held in Mr May's barn on 1 June 1949, where it was decided that as attention had been given to plans and a building licence for the Club room some work could now be done. It was decided to start the following Friday, and that materials be purchased through Mr Gotts, of Mundesley, who would deal direct with various firms.

A set-back was reported at the General Meeting on 27 September 1949, when it was stated that because of a shortage of bricks and labour, the new building was not progressing as fast as had been hoped, but as harvest was nearly over, there would perhaps now be more progress.

The next General Meeting on 7 November 1949 saw arrangements being made for a whist drive to be held on 25 November. Mr W. Wild would be MC, and several members offered to get prizes. Mr May would try to get poultry for a raffle, and Mr A. Hooker would provide some of the refreshments with the Club members paying 6d each towards the rest of the cost.

It was also decided that more money would have to be raised for the building fund to fulfil the cost of building the new Club Room.

At the General Meeting on 23 January 1950, more fund raising events were planned, including a fête to be held at Knapton House and a whist drive. It was suggested by Mr May (who was in the chair, because Rev. Prichard was unable to attend) that all who could should visit the new building on the following Saturday, at 2 p.m. to see if members had any new ideas about the development of the building.

At the next meeting on 8 March 1950, it was reported that the Secretary and Mr Fisher had been to see, and had bought bus seats at 17/6 each, which Mr May had heard about. All agreed that it was a good bargain.

The club finances so far just about balanced, with still more minor items which had to be paid off. The Club still had to keep on making money as more things would have to be bought, even when the building was finished. So a whist drive and barn dance were organised, and a pig was to be the main attraction for a raffle draw.

At meeting held in May 1950, lighting was discussed, and how electricity could be got to the building. The exterior painting of the Club would be brown and cream, and interior cream and green. The dado and below to the skirting would be green as near to the colour of the billiard cloth as possible. The skirting would be done in tiles (timber being short after the war), so it was decided to tile in the main room, darts room and porch, and also to get lino for the floor. The best quality would cost £13 from Mr Cubitt at North Walsham. Three dozen cups and saucers were also bought.

At the General Meeting on 10 August 1950, Mr May presiding, it was stated that the room was nearly completed, and to notify Smallburgh Council of the opening date, which it was hoped would be in the first week of September.

A billiards exhibition was arranged for October 3 in the new Club Room for Marcus Owen, boy billiards champion, and his brother. Invitations were given to each club which had played in the Alby Billiards League. Rev. Prichard and Mr May offered their cars for transport on the night to collect the boys from North Walsham Railway Station, and tea would take place in the darts room for them, with the exhibition starting at 7 p.m. A collection was made in the room to cover the expenses of that evening.

A General Meeting was held in the new Club Room on 25 September 1950. At this Miss Robinson was elected Life President, as it was because of her that the Club had got to where it was now. Vice Presidents were Mr James and Mr Cargill, chairman Mr May, secretary Mr H. Wild, treasurer Mr Claydon, Billiards Captain Mr R. Wright, and Darts Captain Mr G. Wild. The Club was to be open on weekday nights, and if needed by 1 or 2 members on a Saturday, the oil stove only to be used for heating then.

Mrs H. Wild was the cleaner, and it included lighting a fire on weekday nights in the room and at home matches on a Thursday, preparing the refreshments, normally cheese rolls, and making the tea at home in a big urn, which was brought up from her house at the cross roads between 8 and 9 p.m. by two club members. Mr Wild saw to the ironing and brushing of the billiard table. Subscriptions were the first week, one shilling, and the following weeks in the winter season 6d per week, plus 3d per week in the summer season. The fund raising carried on with another whist drive on 13 October 1950.

At a General Meeting in March 1951, Miss Leather, with Miss Robinson, attended, and Miss Leather offered to make curtains for the Club Room. It was agreed that she should make the choice of material she thought most suitable.

In the 1951/2 season fund raising continued, and Mr Guyton donated the Guyton Challenge Cup to be played for each season by American Billiards Tournaments. Winners would hold the cup at home during the summer months if they wished, and it would be on display during the winter. Work was still being carried on by members, with the grass cleared and shingle put down in the front entrance. Each side of the door, a flower bed was made, and on both sides of the front entrance gardens of shrubs, which included two trees planted for Queen Elizabeth the Second's Coronation in 1953.

In later years members voluntarily met to maintain the outside, hedge-cutting, keeping the grounds tidy, and also painting the exterior of the Club Room. Whist Drives were replaced by Bingo in the Parish Room, with members again donating prizes, and with Mrs Stubley and Mrs Pardon serving the refreshments. Donations were made in 1954 to the Playing Field Fund, and in 1961 to the Mrs Johnson Memorial Fund.

In the 1960s, when Mr May, the first of the original Trustees passed away, Mr S. Wright was elected until he moved away from the village. Members took turns in cleaning the room and doing the refreshments on match night when Mrs H. Wild retired as cleaner.

Mr William· Wild, Trustee, passed away in 1993, and Mr Henry Wild, the last of the original Trustees, passed away on 21 October, 2005.

JANET MUNRO (STEWARD)

A chapel childhood and a favourite uncle

Some people can recount in great detail stories of their early childhood and schooldays - not me! I have difficulty remembering what happened yesterday never mind 60 odd years ago.

However, I have done my best to put together a few of my memories of Knapton Chapel. At the same time I have written a piece about my uncle, Arthur Amis; he was a very important person in my life, from my birth right up until his death in 2000, and memories of him I treasure.

It's just occurred to me how strange life is. When I was a baby I lived with my uncle and aunt because my mother was ill. Much later, I in my turn helped to look after them both towards the end of their lives when they needed caring for.

I was born October 1940 to Ellen (née Amis) formerly of Trunch and James Steward of Knapton. My father worked for Norman May at Church Farm and we lived in a farm cottage in Pond Road, quite close to the Methodist Chapel. My father had been born in the same cottage in 1910.

'The Methodist Church in Knapton began in a barn. It formed part of a smallholding and was adjoined to a farm cottage. For a time the barn was used for a carpenter's shop.

In 1880 a retired minister, Rev. E. S. Shields bought the building and adjoining cottage. He came to live in the cottage, turning the barn into a chapel. He made a connecting doorway and had the place registered for worship: licence No. 25155.'

The above is a quotation from *Knapton Celebrates 100 Years of Methodism 1890–1990*, a short history compiled by Herbert S. Hicks. There is no record of what happened between 1880 and 1890.

A further quotation from Herbert's booklet says,

'About 1946 the Young Laymen's League gave some special evening services. One of the results was that a newly wed young man became a member. For many years he and his wife, Mr & Mrs James Steward, were a great blessing. They brought all their family through the chapel and many of them still serve in other churches.'

My mother came from a 'chapel' family so it was obvious that I and any siblings I might have would be brought up to attend the Methodist Church.

This we did, three times on a Sunday. Sunday School in the morning and Chapel Services in the afternoon (2.30 p.m.) and evening (6.30 p.m.)

Often the local preacher would stay to tea, having been 'planned' to preach at both services. We never rebelled against this; it was something that 'was done'.

Of all the local preachers who stayed to tea with us on a Sunday we had our favourites. Mr Brindid from Hickling was liked by all of us - his son Michael went on to publish books in the Norfolk dialect.

I looked forward to Frank Osborne, another preacher from Hickling because he always played games with us; by then I had a sister Ruth and a brother Eric. Frank Ling from North Walsham was another favourite of mine but the most favourite of all was Arthur Amis from Trunch - my mother's brother and our uncle. He was an excellent story teller - more about him later.

Knapton Chapel had a thriving Sunday school when I was young, run by Mr Herbert Hicks and Miss Ursula Fawkes along with several other Sunday school teachers. Mr Hicks was Sunday School Superintendent at our chapel for more than forty years.

Each year we would enter scripture examinations, we all passed with flying colours every time and we were so proud to receive our certificates at the end of the exams. We learned great chunks of the Bible off by heart, and just like the times tables learned at school these things remain forever.

I cannot get used to the newer versions of the Bible, the words I learned sixty odd years ago have stayed with me. The modern versions are not for me.

We had a Christian Endeavour meeting every Tuesday evening at 6.30 p.m., which was always well attended.

Once a year the North Walsham Methodist Circuit held an Eisteddfod - a local festival for musical competitions etc. All the chapels entered, both adults and children with singing, recitations, bible readings and art amongst other things. It was always very competitive.

Each year at chapel we had our Sunday School Anniversary. Everyone learned a recitation as well as solos and duets that we performed for our families. The chapel was always full and all the girls had new dresses.

At Christmas time we had lovely parties in the Parish Room, (now called the Village Hall). And in the summer time there was the Sunday school treat to Yarmouth. We went by coach and it seemed to take forever to get there. I thought Yarmouth was hundreds of miles away - not just 30 minutes down the road (by today's travelling standards). Mum and Dad always took us to the circus. I used to love the ending, the floor sank and the ring filled with water, ducks and geese swam in, the dancing girls were wearing sparkling costumes and there were fountains and coloured lights, I thought it was magic

Knapton Chapel still has a Sunday School today although this tends to be the exception rather than the rule.

Looking back now I count myself fortunate to have been brought up the way I was - my childhood revolved around home, school and chapel and as far as I can remember it was a happy childhood.

I still have connections with the chapel being a member of Knapton Woman's Own - a group that began over 50 years ago - founded by my mother (Ellen Steward) and Herbert Hick's wife (Margaret Hicks). I must mention here that Margaret is still a member, holding the office of Programme Secretary, a post she has held from the beginning. In April of this year, 2007, she will be celebrating her 93rd birthday.

Now back to Uncle Arthur! - Along with his many years as a Methodist Local Preacher he was also, at various times, a Parish, District and County Councillor

He started off his working life as a cowman at Hill Farm in Mundesley, immediately joining the National Union of Agricultural

Workers. He was very active in the union and helped to marshal their forces in the 1926 General Strike.

His autobiography *From Dawn to Dusk* is now held in research libraries, including the House of Commons, as a reference work on rural bygone life.

In 1958 he became the first secretary-agent for the North Norfolk Labour Party, firstly serving Edwin Gooch MP and then Bert Hazell MP.

Of all the things he did in his long life - he died February 25th 2000 aged 92 years - the most important as far as this piece is concerned is that Arthur Amis was once a pupil of Knapton School.

Mundesley 2007

Some members of the 1949 Knapton Sports Team in April 2007

Left to right: Shirley Wright, Jill Watts, Yvonne Lee, Barbara Dixon, Willie Puncher, Janet Steward, Margaret Wild, Michael Miller

Part 5
ANNEX A

Letter

KNAPTON SCHOOL 1932 TO 1961

A small group of former pupils of Knapton School are anxious to collect memories of the school and of the village, before we all get too old to remember! We have chosen the period between 1932 and 1961, because that was the time that Mrs. Johnson was head of the school, and because we had to draw a line somewhere. Memories before and after those years will obviously also be welcome.

We are Janet Munro (formerly Steward), Kathleen Suckling (formerly Johnson) and Gillian Shephard (formerly Watts).

We have produced a questionnaire so that we can make sure that all those who choose to take part give the same basis of information, and also a long list of suggestions to jog all our memories.

If you would like to help, and want to talk over the idea, do please ring Janet, Kathleen, Gillian, or Richard and June Wild.

Not everyone will want to write a long essay, but if enough are interested, we hope to organise a reunion in Knapton Parish Hall in the spring, so that people who would rather talk about their memories can have the chance to do so instead of writing. It would be good to meet up anyway.

You may be wondering what will be done with all this material. Gillian thinks that if we collect enough we could get it published. But we need the material first, so do please help if you are interested.

If you do want to help, please complete the questionnaire, and write down anything, however short, you remember about your time at Knapton School. We all look forward to hearing from you.

QUESTIONNAIRE

Please fill in as much of the questionnaire as you can.

Name   Maiden name
Date of Birth
Address   Tel. no.
                                         email if any

Years at Knapton School between ....and
Address while a pupil at Knapton School...........................
Family
Father's occupation
Mother's occupation (she may have worked in the home)
Brothers and sisters   names and dates of birth

Did you have grandparents living in Knapton? If not, where did they live?

Which school/college/university did you attend after Knapton School?

Please give details of your subsequent career

Did you and/or your family attend Knapton Church, the Methodist Chapel, or the Catholic Church?

Which members of your family did active service (including Home Guard and ARP) during the war?

Were you a member of the Boys Brigade, the GFS, or other organisation?

Did you do any special jobs at home, like getting water in? Or part time jobs, like delivering the papers, or helping on the farm?

Below we have listed a series of 'memory joggers' to help you remember things about Knapton School, about Knapton itself, and about the period between 1932 and 1961.

If you want to write about any of the things listed, or anything else, please do so. It does not matter how briefly you write, everything will be of interest.

1. Knapton School - the building
The big room
The little room
The kitchen
The cloakrooms
The outside lavatories
The bike shed and playground
The garden, and individual school gardens
Furniture - desks and chairs
Equipment - the gramophone, the piano, PE equipment (hoops, mats, balls). Anything else

2. The people
Mrs Johnson
Mrs Woodage (Miss Doughty)
Miss Collier
Mrs Breeze
Mr Featherstone
Mrs Featherstone
Any other teachers that you remember

Mrs Watts (the cleaner)
Miss Townsend (the dinner lady)
Any other people who regularly worked in the school
Mrs Watling, who cooked dinners

3. Visitors to Knapton School
The attendance man (Mr Reeve)
The dentist
The doctor
The school nurse
The dinner man from Bacton
Anyone else

4. Lessons
Which were your favourite lessons and why?
Lessons from the radio e.g. Singing Together, How Things Began, the Radio Doctor, PE and Games
Practical work, like sewing, knitting, woodwork, fretwork
Anything else

The Scholarship

5. The School Year
Christmas - making decorations
            Stencils, School gardens
Picking the pinks
Harvest - did you have to help?

6. Milk and school dinners - What do you remember?

7. Getting to school
How did you get there e.g. walk, cycle, bus? How long did it take you?

8. Outings and visits
Cromer, London, Blakeney Point, Great Yarmouth
Sports days at North Walsham
Singing or country dancing festivals in other schools

KNAPTON VILLAGE

Can you remember anything about
The Church
The Chapel
The Men's club
The WI
Sunday School
The Chapel Youth Group
The shop

When did electricity come to the village? How did your mother cook before that?
When did running water and sewerage come to the village?
What were the arrangements for water and lavatories before that?
Where did your family do the shopping?
What meal did you consider to be a real treat?
Did you have a garden or allotment?
Did you keep a pig, rabbits, ferrets, chickens, dogs, cats, guinea pigs etc.?
What jobs did you have at home, like collecting rabbit food or gardening?
Can you remember anything about food rationing in the war? Can you remember eating your first banana, or ice cream?
What village occasions do you remember? e.g. fêtes, socials, village parties, weddings?

If you lived in another village, like Paston, Mundesley, or Edingthorpe, please do add anything you remember about living there.

LIFE AND TIMES

What events do you remember e.g.
The outbreak of the Second World War
The end of the Second World War
The death of King George VI
Food rationing
The end of food rationing
The snow in 1947
The floods in 1953
The first combine harvester
Can you remember steam threshing? Where did it take place in Knapton?

A typical school report from 1956

ANNEX B

Participants

	First name	Family name	Married Name	Period at School	Q.No	Account
1	Philip	Almey		1946 - 1947	Q	
2	Queenie	Bane	Wild	1922 - 1930	Q	AC
3	Ivy	Burlingham	Austin	1938 - 1947	Q	
4	Grace	Burlingham	Ellis	1942 - 1948	Q	
5	Andrew	Claydon		1957 - 1963	Q	AC
6	Neville	Coe		1954 - 1960	Q	
7	Jackie	Croxon	Elvin	1948 - 1952		AC
8	Pamela	Dixon	Garnham	1946 - 1949	Q	AC
9	Roger	Dixon		1939 - 1945	Q	AC
10	Nellie	Dixon	Kirk	1928 - 1934	Q	AC
11	Barbara	Dixon	Jarvis	1946 - 1952		AC
12	Mervyn	Fawkes		1933 - 1942	Q	AC
13	Roy	Fawkes		1934 - 1944	Q	AC
14	Gordon	Harrison		1948 - 1957		AC
15	Pearl	Hicks	Eves	1956 - 1962		AC
16	Kathleen	Johnson	Suckling	1941 - 1948	Q	AC
17	Maureen	Kirk	Stubley	1951 - 1958	Q	AC
18	Ellen May (Nellie)	Kirk	Dixon (Deceased)	1928 - 1934		AC
19	Llewelleyn	Kirk		1935 - 1941	Q	AC
20	Josephine	Langham	Hourahane	1944 - 1945	Q	AC
21	Edward	Langham		1944 - 1945		AC
22	Yvonne	Lee	Chambers	1944 - 1953	Q	
23	Ann	Lee	Isitt	1941 - 1947	Q	AC
24	David	Lee		1941 -1947		AC
25	Joy	Lee		1935 - 1944		AC
26	Phyllis	Meffin	Brewer	1934 - 1941	Q	
27	Sam	Meffin		1936 - 194	Q	
28	Michael	Miller		1943 - 1957	Q	
29	Ray	Pearman		1936 - 1942	Q	
30	Barbara	Puncher	Emm	1947 - 1956	Q	
31	Willie	Puncher		1942 - 1951	Q	AC
32	Joan	Puncher	Jones	1949 - 1957	Q	
33	John	Rayner		1946 - 1950		AC
34	Jacqueline	Skippen	Slipper	1952 - 1955	Q	
35	Ruth	Steward	Matthew	1947 - 1953	Q	
36	Mary	Steward	Lewis	1954 - 1960	Q	
37	Janet	Steward	Munro	1944 - 1954	Q	AC
38	William	Stubley		1955 - 1957	Q	
39	Josephine (Josie)	Watts	Graham	1948 - 1956	Q	AC
40	Gillian	Watts	Shephard	1945 - 1951	Q	AC
41	David	White		1954 - 1960	Q	AC
42	Sylva	White		1955 - 1960	Q	
43	Dorothy	Wild	Madeley	1925 - 1934	Q	AC
44	June	Wild	Wild	1956 - 1962	Q	AC
45	Malcolm	Wild		1948 - 1954	Q	AC

46	Brian	Wild		1946 - 1955	Q	AC
47	Richard	Wild		1951 - 1957	Q	AC
48	Brenda	Wilkins		1946 - 1952	Q	
49	Shirley	Wright	Conquest	1943 - 1952	Q	AC
50	John	Wright		1946 - 1955	Q	AC
51	Cecil	Yaxley		1947 - 1957	Q	
52	Crystal	Thompson	Pye	1951 - 1958		AC
53	John	Wright		1946 - 1955	Q	AC
54	Alfred	Yaxley	(Deceased)	1905 - 1914		AC
55	Phyllis	Ashley		1928 - 1938	A	
56	Linda	Fawkes	Risebrow	1955 - 1961	A	
57	Rene	Fawkes	Turner	1956 - 1963	A	
58	Ronald	Fawkes		1931 - 1940	A	
59	Tony	Leeder		1943 - 1951	A	
60	Arthur	Lubbock		1934 - 1948	A	
61	Mary	Puncher	Steward	1953 - 1960	A	
62	William	Schamp		1958 - 1968	A	
63	Reggie	Smith		1937 - 1947	A	
64	Eric	Steward		1949 - 1957	A	
65	Jennifer	Wild	Lambert	1948 -1960	A	
66	Margaret	Wild	Bane	1944 - 1955	A	
67	Barbara	Wilkins	Fawkes	1936 - 1942	A	

ANNEX C

Occupations

Those who completed the questionnaires and in some cases, provided written accounts gave details of their fathers' and mothers' occupations, and of their own subsequent careers.

Name	Parents' occupations	Own career
Philip Almey	Farmers	Farmer
Queenie Bane	Father farm labourer	Domestic
Grace Burlingham	Father farm manager Mother home and farm work	Nanny, boatyard work, Care assistant
Ivy Burlingham	Parents as above	Housewife, hairdresser
Andrew Claydon	Father farmer	Tenant farmer
Neville Coe	Father gardener, road man Mother home help	Boat builder, Bacton gas site
Pamela Dixon	Father poultry farmer Mother shop and post office	Sub post mistress guest house owner
Barbara Dixon	Parents as above	Fashion retail
Roger Dixon	Father motor mechanic Mother daily help, farm work	Teacher, curate, vicar, rural dean
Nellie Dixon	Father gardener Mother pub licensee	School cleaner, Dinner lady
Mervyn Fawkes	Father gardener Mother seasonal fruit picking	Apprentice carpenter, coach driver
Roy Fawkes	Parents as above	Motor mechanic and coach Driver
Gordon Harrison	Father station master	Building trades
Kathleen Johnson Mother head teacher	Father poultry farmer Mother head teacher	Home economics teacher

Llewellyn Kirk	Farm worker and gardener	Coach builder, and Carpenter
Maureen Kirk	Father agricultural engineer Mother dinner lady	Banking, Barclays, HSBC
Josephine Langham	Father Dental technician Mother, various jobs	Teacher
Edward Langham	As above	Director, Canadian Space Agency
Anne Lee	Mother a widow	Teacher
Phyllis Meffin	Father farm worker	
Sam Meffin	As above	Crane driver etc
Michael Miller	Father farm worker	Agricultural worker
Ray Pearman	Father cowman	Cowman
Willie Puncher	Father farmer	Farmer
Barbara Puncher	Father engineering works Farm work, gas site	Catering assistant
Joan Puncher	As above	School cook
John Rayner	Father painter and decorator	University Professor
Jacqueline Skippen	Father painter and decorator	Secretarial work
Ruth Steward	Father farm worker Mother house work for others	Nursery nurse
Mary Steward	as above	Child care
Janet Steward	as above	Residential care Children, aged, Homeless

Willian Stubley	Father a stockman Mother a cook	Royal Navy and MOD consultant
Gillian Watts	Father cattle dealer and poultry farmer	Teacher, M.P Minister, Peer
Josephine Watts	Father a carpenter	Secretarial, and shop manager
Dorothy Wild	Father a gardener	Shop work, Nursing, Councillor
June Wild	Father a carpenter Mother a cleaner	Hairdresser
Brian Wild	Father farm worker Mother domestic work	Gardening, Newspaper round
Richard Wild	As above	Bricklayer
Malcolm Wild	Father a farm worker Mother domestic work	Police officer
David White	Father pigman, and builder's Labourer	Norwich Union
Sylvia White	As above	Land work, then Work
Brenda Wilkins	Teamman	Shop work, then Service
Shirley Wright	Father a farm worker	Secretarial, then Registrar of births, Marriages and deaths
John Wright	Father a farm worker	Carpenter and builder
Cecil Yaxley	Father a farm worker Mother domestic work	RAF

KNAPTON

CELEBRATES 100 YEARS OF METHODISM

1890 to 1990

A Short History

Compiled

by

Herbert S Hicks

KNAPTON CELEBRATES

ONE HUNDRED YEARS OF METHODISM

1890 - 1990

The Methodist Church in Knapton began in a barn. It formed part of a small holding and was adjoined to a farm cottage. For a time the barn was used for a carpenter's shop.

In 1880 a retired minister, Rev. E.S. Shields, bought the building and adjoining cottage. He came to live in the cottage, turning the barn into a chapel. He made a connecting doorway and had the place registered for wor-ship: licence No. 25155.

We have no record of what happened in the next ten years.

In the year 1890 the North Walsham Primitive Methodist Circuit hired the buildings and began organising services. A rent of £2 per year was paid. The minister's name was Rev. I. Buck.

The circuit contributed 15/- per quarter to help the society get started.

In 1896 Rev. G.W. Hancock became minister. The records show that coal was 1/2d per cwt. Oil for the lamps was 9d per gallon. There was an open fire-place in the south wall.

It appears that services were discontinued in 1902, but someone carried on paying the rent.

In 1916 the chapel re-opened. A new head teacher, name of Miss Carpenter, came to the school house, with her mother. They were keen to have services re-started.

More improvements were made to the building. A wooden porch was built inside the west wall. A wooden floor was laid, and a tortoise stove placed in the centre of the chapel. A new hymn board was also made.

Mrs Carpenter died in 1930. Her daughter, the Knapton School head teacher, with other members had a plate of remembrance placed on the east wall. It included several who had passed on to their reward during the previous few years: Georgina Wright, J.W. Scott, John Roberts, Janet Carpenter, William Watts, Philip Appleton.

167

By 1935 Knapton Methodists were able to contribute a little to the circuit (£2 per quarter), as well as paying £5 per year off the loan.

In 1937 I married a Knapton member and came to live in the village. The Knapton Chapel was not then licensed for marriages. So we were married at the Wesleyan Chapel at Trunch by Rev. T. Featherstone. The new chapel at Trunch was being built, but was not complete.

I then transferred my membership from Trunch to Knapton, and Mr Featherstone asked me to become Trust treasurer and Sunday School superintendent. At that time there were five scholars and seven chapel members. There were no trustees living in Knapton. Most of the few still living were in North Walsham. Owing to the war none were present for the first three yearly meetings.

1944 brought many changes. The existing porch was built, the doorway to the adjoining cottage blocked off, and the inside wooden porch removed. At the disposal of the Trimingham Chapel Knapton bought the seats. The pulpit was bought and given by two devoted members, Mr and Mrs James Bowman.

The tortoise stove was removed and the seats fixed in place. Up to this time the seating arrangements consisted of four chairs, making up the front row, and five rows of wooden forms. These forms had one rail running along the back. So if you were very short or went to sleep you could fall through. A new entrance was built, with a brick arch. Owing to bomb damage during the war years the government paid out 8/- per year for five years.

A new trust was formed in 1945. This included more local persons, able to give better support and guidance.

About 1946 the Y.L.L. (Young Laymen's League) gave some special evening services. One of the results was that a newly wed young man became a member. For many years he and his wife, Mr & Mrs James Steward, were a great blessing. They brought all their family through the chapel and many of them still serve in other churches.

In 1947 electricity was installed, costing £17. In 1951 the water was laid on.

In 1955 we suffered the loss of a very gifted member, Mrs Iris Fawkes. Married in the chapel, she died at the age of only 23 years. Iris's former name was Carr. She had come through the Sunday School and become a teacher, serving also as President of the Women's Own, secretary to the Circuit Youth Council, and secretary to the Circuit Eisteddfod. Her husband presented an oak table, two chairs and the oak communion rail in her memory.

In 1960 the new schoolroom was built, where an old cart shed and stable had stood. (Preachers no longer came by horse and trap).

5 Four years later an electric organ was purchased. In 1970 money was raised to buy a new oak pulpit to replace the old worm-eaten pine one. The pulpit was put in a corner position. A cross on the wall was given central place. Miss Mackenzie presented an oak screen, matching the communion rail, to screen the organ. This she gave in memory of her father, Rev. F. Mackenzie. This completed the lay-out of the front of the church.

By 1979 the congregation had increased and the schoolroom was very much used by youth activities, committee meetings, Women's Own, Parish Council, Men's Fellowship, Parish Church Council meetings, etc. So it was felt that a kitchen and toilet were badly needed. We had no land around our buildings, but Mr & Mrs Hammond, local farmers, offered us, for a nominal fee, a small part of a garden from his cottage land adjoining our schoolroom at the north end of the chapel. We were very grateful for this kind gesture and began to plan ways and means to build.

It was estimated that the cost would be around £10,000. Fortunately we still owned the cottage at the south end of the chapel. It was in a deplorable condition and had been empty for some years. We decided to sell it and use the proceeds of sale. It made £6000. To our delight it was bought by a young Methodist minister, Rev. L. Osborn, and his wife.

About this time we experienced some very severe weather. Water and snow came through the chapel roof and flooded the floor. The roof had to be re-tiled, the walls re-decorated, and new carpet laid. Fortunately the insurance company shared the costs. This task completed, we focussed our attention on building the kitchen and toilet. The project was finished in 1985 and we now find it most useful.

We have a very happy, loving fellowship in our society today. There are twenty four members, six under 20 years old. There are fifteen children, Women's Own has 25 members, and Men's Fellowship fifteen members. We have a monthly Prayer Circle, and regular united worship and other shared activities with our friends in the Parish Church.

We praise God for all that is past and trust that the future may be fruitful and bring glory to His Name.

Part 6

The Last Word

a poem written by Deryck Featherstone, just before he died in February 2007. Mr Featherstone was the husband of Joyce Featherstone, who taught the infants at Knapton School for many years. He himself also taught at Knapton for a brief period.

COASTAL MEMORIES

Summer sun in Wells
Gone are boyhood dreams but the magic lingers
A wall on the quay
Fish and Chips
Blue-green Blakeney marshes,
Endless, featureless, Man is the intruder.
Rain on the northerly gale, icy, stinging,
Breathtaking, clean, pure
Sky-darkening numberless birds over Cley
Swirling, swooping, circling, organized,
ignoring gulls and bread-feeding ducks.
Who controls their landing path?
Food for all in the black mud, they say.
Come down feathered friends and fill your beaks,
stale bread and crusts for ducks,
Ices for the kids.
Gorse and heather on Weybourne heath, feast your eyes.
Hear the distant whistle as engines toil to Holt.
Shops at Sheringham, crowds and Cromer crabs,
Fishermen's voices, a race apart.

Soft Norfolk accents still surviving; grey flint towers, can you count them?
Village chapels 'where two or three are gathered together'.
Yet still survives the hearty singing of Wesley's Hymns
And 'The Word' is proclaimed

Smiling faces behind the check-out where it's a pleasure to shop,
Crowded pavements where Mums find time to chat,
Two 'old boys' in an unspoilt pub stop for a pint and a mardle

Dappled leaves freshly rained-on, good brown earth freshly tilled,
Distant tractors, giant combines, golden cornfields.
Newcomers, incomers, weekenders why do you come?
Why bor, cos thass Norfolk, thass why.

Deryck Featherstone 18th February 2007

171